HOW TO ACE YOUR JOB INTERVIEW

Sudhir Andrews

INDIA • SINGAPORE • MALAYSIA

ISBN 979-8-89133-637-7

Contents

A Letter from the Author

Dear Job Hunter,

Oh dear! There you are with sweaty palms and a sinking feeling in your belly. You have just been grilled by the interviewer. They threw questions at you left and right, and you spluttered an answer, knowing that you could have done better. The reactions on the interviewer's face showed they were unimpressed. How unfortunate when you know you are right for the job.

They offered you a limp hand in disinterest when they said goodbye at the office door. You drive back home, pounding the car steering wheel, wondering, "Why did I say that?" The damage is done. You will never hear back. You find out later that the job did go to someone else, even though you had a better resume. But unknown to you, that person had polished their job interview skills. If only you knew the right words to say to their questions, that job would have been yours.

But don't despair, dear reader. What if I told you that you can ace your next interview by mastering job interview skills found in this book, which will make you look forward to interviews rather than being tense and insecure?

I promise to potentially double or triple your odds of getting the job. This book empowers you with answers typically asked by candidates:

- How do I overcome interview jitters?
- How can I make a positive impression?
- How do I prepare for an interview?
- How do I prepare a hotshot resume?

- What should I wear for the interview?
- How do I deal with different types of interviews?
- What kind of questions can I expect?
- Why does the interviewer ask certain questions?
- What kind of answers can I give?
- How can I counter the interviewer's style of questioning?
- What kind of questions can I ask the interviewer?
- How can I make telephone interviews a success?
- What if I am an average candidate?
- How can I negotiate a better salary?
- What happens after the interview?

This book has it all! I am empowering you with 101 most popularly asked questions and how to answer them. You can dramatically increase your odds of winning at the job interview. The book unlocks the secrets of success.

But first, why did I write this book for you? For two reasons:

In my 30 years of interviewing, I was appalled at the lack of preparation by candidates, and even though I favoured them for selection, they ruined their chances. I want to give you insight from the other side of the table.

I wrote the first edition of this book in 1988 as a companion to candidates when they prepared for interviews. I have been deeply encouraged by the readers over the years. I have upgraded the book to introduce the changes in modern times as well as bring in international perspectives. You are now a global citizen, and the world is your job market.

As a starter, let us refresh ourselves with some basics:

WHAT IS AN INTERVIEW?

An interview is an opportunity to present yourself for selection. Interviews have become an essential and critical part of your life. This is especially true in our competitive world where selectors have numerous candidates to choose from, and the interview becomes the means of differentiating you from another. But here is a secret! The market may be full of candidates, but few succeed at interviews because they just do not prepare for them. I am sure that you, the reader, would like to be one of the successful ones.

WHY ARE WE NERVOUS ABOUT INTERVIEWS?

Our first interview was at the impressionable age of four or five when we went for admission to a nursery school. Most of us remember it as a frightening experience because of the new environment, new faces, and, above all, the separation from the warmth and comfort of our parents' presence. Our parents may have thought us naïve, but in fact, we sensed their anxiety along with the cries of other children and the hustle and bustle so unnatural to us. The confusing situation may have planted the seeds of the fear of interviews. Consequently, interviews have become a much-dreaded thing.

We continued to face interviews throughout our school life, especially the dreaded parent-teacher meeting where our progress report was discussed. We faced interviews when changing schools. But here's some news: the succession of interviews will never end. It continues when getting admission into a college, with the banker to get a loan, with the government for permissions and licences, with the tax authorities regarding tax deductions, with organisations to get jobs, etc. **The most important interview is the one for a job, which is what this book is all about.**

What makes interviews daunting is the fear of failure. Obviously, interviews are held for something that will significantly influence our lives. Failure in an interview is humiliating, shameful, and a blow to our self-esteem. Success in an interview brings pride to us, our family, community, neighbourhood, or alma mater.

Naturally, we would like to succeed. While there are coaching schools for written tests such as GMAT, TOEFL, JEEs, etc., there are few that prepare you for an interview. Wouldn't you like to know the secrets to succeed at interviews? This book does just that.

I wish readers happy reading and success in your future interviews.

Sudhir Andrews

One

Concept of Mutuality

The Oxford Dictionary defines an interview as a face-to-face meeting, especially for the purpose of obtaining a statement or assessing the qualities of a candidate. 'Interview' is derived from the French word "entrevoir," which means 'glimpse.' This, therefore, indicates a physical meeting of people with certain possible objectives:

1. To obtain a statement or opinion – as is done when film stars are interviewed to get their views on a role, or when a prime minister is interviewed to get a statement on a political issue.
2. To assess a person for selection – such as interviews for jobs, admission to an educational institution, or getting a bank loan.
3. By a doctor to assess a patient's complaint.

This book is concerned with the second objective, with special reference to interviews for jobs.

PURPOSE OF A JOB INTERVIEW

The purpose of an interview is to create an opportunity for people to meet and converse with each other on a matter of mutual benefit. The participants consist of one or more interviewers who pose questions concerning the objective of the job interview to an interviewee who answers them. But there is a significant difference that people often forget or do not know: the interviewee can also ask questions. Therein lies the concept of mutuality, where both partners benefit. Most candidates believe that they are subjected to a barrage of questions, when in fact they have an equal right to ask questions too. A successful interview cannot be a one-way street. The belief that an interview is a one-way street causes the fear of the interview because the candidate feels judged, when in fact they can also evaluate the suitability of a job or organisation. The interview is an occasion for discussion where both sides decide the future course of action. In job interviews, the organisation, interviewer(s), and interviewee are stakeholders (those who benefit from a process). Let us examine in detail how they gain from an interview:

HOW THE ORGANISATION BENEFITS

The success of any organisation depends on its people. An organisation may have expensive assets, extensive facilities, and efficient systems and processes. However, their successful use is in the hands of the right people. These individuals must possess the right knowledge, skills, and competencies to meet the organisation's objectives. Therefore, one of the main concerns for an organisation is to have the right person for the right job. The interview helps the organisation select the right person for a given vacancy. Those assigned the task of recruitment are challenged to make the right selection.

An organisation invests significant sums of money in recruitment and selection processes. First, there are the prohibitive costs of job advertisements or fees to recruitment agencies. Second, there is the cost of the time of the interviewers. Third, there is the cost of travel for interviewers to conduct out-of-town interviews. Fourth, there are the costs associated with hiring a place for the interview. Finally, there are the costs of reimbursing candidates for their travel expenses. organisations are under pressure to make these investments productive by selecting the right people who will ultimately contribute to achieving the organisation's goals and bring returns to the organisation.

Sometimes, a job vacancy takes several months to fill. This ***lead time*** represents a loss to the organisation as the position remains unproductive without the right person. During the interview, the organisation must ensure that the wait was well worth it.

HOW THE INTERVIEWER BENEFITS

The interviewer is often the Human Resources Manager, Functional Head, and, in the case of senior positions, a member of the Board. An interview takes them away from their regular job duties, and they are very conscious of the time they spend at the interview. This time must be productive as it could have been allocated to other pressing tasks. Throughout my career, I have often encountered challenges in assembling an interview panel due to the valuable man-hours interviews consume.

An interviewer's skill in conducting interviews is thoroughly tested during the process. Interviewing skills are fundamental to most positions that involve responsibility and accountability. Interviewers, therefore, hold crucial roles within an organisation. To fail in making the right selections would mean falling short of fulfilling their responsibilities. This pressure demands that they remain mentally alert, be effective listeners, and ask the right questions. They also need to possess the right motivational skills to persuade a strong candidate to choose their organisation when candidates have multiple options. So, here's a surprise: interviewers experience nervousness just like you do during an interview.

HOW THE CANDIDATE BENEFITS

The primary motivation for an interviewee is the hope of being selected, which can lead to enriching life experiences, achieving status, and enjoying a better quality of life. Interviews are pursued with the aim of securing something better than the current situation.

Another significant aspect for a candidate is their own self-esteem. Success in an interview boosts self-esteem and subsequently enhances their overall sense of well-being. Often, there are multiple candidates vying for the same position, creating competition. Success in the interview instils self-confidence and a belief in being better than others. It also brings pride to the candidate's family, neighbourhood, and alma mater. It's common to hear students proudly boasting about the success of their seniors who have achieved important positions.

By now, we've recognised that all parties involved have important stakes in interviews. It logically follows that interviews can be most beneficial when approached with a mindset of mutuality. Everyone has needs during an interview, and the best approach is one of partnership where the rights of each party are respected, and there is a free exchange of information. Just as the organisation and interviewer seek information about you, you also have the right to gather information about the job and the organisation. You want to determine whether joining the organisation is convenient for you. For example, a BPO may have a vacancy for night shifts only, which may not suit many candidates.

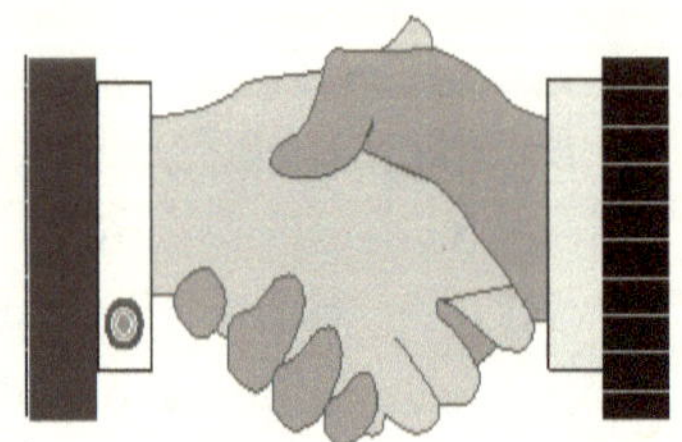

Unfortunately, many individuals forfeit their rights during interviews due to the belief that job opportunities are scarce and hard to come by. The essence of the interview experience is closely tied to your mindset. If your attitude is geared toward exercising your rights, then the interview takes on a tone of mutuality, becomes less intimidating, and has a greater chance of success. I recall several candidates withdrawing their candidature because the terms and conditions of employment did not suit them. Others withdrew because the job content did not align with their skills and competencies, while many declined offers due to issues related to pay. Many candidates regret joining organisations within the first month because they did not exercise their right during the interview to gather more information about the organisation, working conditions, and the job itself. For instance, one individual hastily joined the back processing unit of a bank, only to discover that she had to work 12 hours a day, sometimes even on weekends, without receiving overtime pay or consideration for meals and transportation home after late hours. She left the job within one month!

I'm certain you would like to know the questions that you should ask during an interview. You can find these questions in Chapter 9, "101 Frequently Asked Questions." However, it's crucial to emphasise that there is no limit to the questions you can ask about the organisation. Ideally, you should have conducted thorough research about the job and the organisation before your interview. This preparation can reduce the number of questions you need to ask during the interview, but it's still essential to confirm any remaining queries at that time. You have every right to seek answers to these questions. Any organisation that does not provide the time and opportunity to address your concerns may not be worth considering in the first place. Furthermore, the manner in which you ask questions is also crucial. Approach your inquiries politely and with dignity, avoiding an arrogant or confrontational tone.

Remember: Good interviewers like candidates who ask questions. They believe that candidates show real interest in the organisation and the job in doing so.

Two

Job Search

I'm sure you'd like to know where to look when seeking a job. There are several sources from which you can find job vacancies:

- The Internet
- Specialty job sites
- Company websites
- The newspaper
- Trade magazines
- Recruitment Agencies
- Employment exchange
- Your college Placement Cell Board

The Internet is loaded with job sites, with more than 4,000 job sites online. Visit large job sites like Monster.com, Jobs.com, Careerbuilder.com, Naukri.com, and TimesJob.com, and check out the 'Help Wanted' bulletin boards. These mega-sites post jobs from around the world, and you're likely to find many listings in your job category. Don't hesitate to submit your resume to these sites. Keep in mind, though, that you'll be competing with four million other candidates! Can you imagine the number of resumes a good posting will generate? If you're fortunate, you may receive a call immediately; otherwise, you may have to wait. The competition for the best jobs can be fierce. If you're a generalist in your profession, these massive sites shouldn't be your first stop in your online search. On the other hand, if you're a nano-technology engineer with a Ph.D. in calculus, which is a specialised field, the competition won't be as intense, since most people aren't familiar with what a nano-technology engineer does!

In either case, it certainly doesn't hurt to sign up with these sites and post your resume. You may receive a call simply because the timing is right, and your stars are properly aligned!

FUNCTIONAL JOB SITES

These sites focus on a particular industry, skill set, or other specific criteria. For example, there are several websites that connect chartered accountants, engineers, hoteliers, etc. Some of these sites are sponsored by professional associations like the Institute of Chartered Accountants, the Federation of the Hotel and Restaurant Associations, the Indian Society for Training and Development, etc. Such sites are tailored to your qualifications and are likely to yield more successful results than general job sites.

Most states have job listings posted in local newspapers. Some include them as part of the primary state website, while others have separate websites dedicated to employment listings. These sites are useful for finding local and regional job openings, especially for job seekers who prefer not to relocate their families across the country. Many of the listings on state job sites are for positions in state government. If you have experience in this area, check out the postings on your state's website or the websites of states where you'd be willing to move.

Additionally, you can post your resume on these government-sponsored sites, which is always a good idea. The right viewer may be searching for someone just like you.

COMPANY WEBSITES

If you are very clear as to a specific company you wish to join, then it is most effective to apply through the company website.

Large companies post job listings on their own sites. Many have a link off the home page labelled 'Job Opportunities', 'Employment', or

'Careers'. These are definitely worth adding to your favourites file during a job search. New postings come up daily, and you can target the job you specifically want.

Many large companies will even e-mail you when openings in your area of expertise are posted. This can be a real time-saver. Most of these sites will create a digital (on-line) resume and keep it in their database. People have received calls months after posting resumes on some company sites. But you never know.

A FEW WORDS OF CAUTION

Looking for a job can be stressful. Unfortunately, a lot of unscrupulous people know this, and online job scams have been reported. So, here are a few tips to protect yourself, your wallet, and your personal information.

1. Never pay a site listing fee. You become a 'commodity' for these sites. Employers should pay all fees and be glad they found you.
2. Never post personal information on an unsecured site. There are all kinds of hackers, crackers, script kiddies, and other cybercreeps who would love to know all about you. Post your resume on secure sites, but never list critical information like your driving licence number, credit card number, Aadhaar card number (Social Security number), or mailing address. Provide an e-mail address only when you post your resume on an open job site.
3. Remove your posted, online resumes from job sites once you've found a job. Again, you already have enough personal information floating through the Ethernet without adding to it.
4. When purchasing from a resume writing or resume submission service, for example, ensure that the information is encrypted before hitting submit.

   Encryption, in short, ensures the private information you submit online is kept safe. In your browser, you can recognise an encrypted form when the root URL starts with "https:" instead of "http:" or see the padlock present in the bottom right corner of your screen. Purchasing from companies with added security measures in place can ensure your private information avoids the hands of ill-willed people.

5. Read and understand the privacy policies of the sites you patronise. Professional organisations possess a strict policy for members who do business online. A privacy statement must be displayed on the company's website; there are no exceptions. Professional organisations value the trust of online applicants. A privacy statement outlines what type of customer information is collected and how it's used. Alliances and partnerships, for example, arrange for Company A to sell or pass on client information to Company B. The information transferred or sold could be basic, like name and email address, or far more in-depth, like name, address, social security number, and phone number. No matter how basic or detailed the information, the company must have the logistics spelled out in their privacy policy.

6. One must be wary of submission invitations. Scammers and spammers follow the same patterns. Mass emails are sent to an enormous list of recipients. Not everyone on the "hit list" is searching for a new job; however, only a small number of people need to be convinced, or tricked into believing, that the email is authentic in order for the scam to be deemed successful. Receiving an email from a recruiter who states, "We saw your resume on the Internet, and we find your skill set to be perfect for one of our clients. Please complete our online application through the below link." Ask yourself a series of questions: Did you send your resume to this recruiter? Visit the company's website (type the web address into your browser; avoid clicking the link in the email); upon further examination, are they reputable? How did they hear about you? Call the company if necessary. Always proceed with caution when you receive a cold-contact email from someone. They could be shams to avoid.

7. Phishing is an attempt to extract personal information through what appear to be authentic emails. If you are job searching, an email from a seemingly interested recruiter may seem normal, and you may consider it legitimate. However, looks can be deceiving.

Knowing what counter checks you need to do protects you from fraud.

8. Avoid responding to requests for personal information, such as a social security or credit card number. Let's say you receive an email from what appears to be a well-known job bank. The email states that they need your account number to update your records. You click on the link, and you're taken to a page that looks, feels, and "smells" right. You proceed by submitting the requested information. The link appeared safe, but you were taken to a site designed to defraud you. Reputable companies will rarely ask for personal information via email, so examine every incoming email for validity. Avoid giving your information out freely. Whether you're at the end of a phishing attack or the job application requires more information than you're willing to provide, proceed with caution. Much like you'll analyse job opportunities, intensely examine each person who receives your personal information. With safe online practices, you'll get the best return from your job-search efforts.

9. Using online job sites offers the opportunity to discover the perfect job that you would never have found using conventional means. It's convenient; employers love them for all sorts of reasons, and they work when used to your best advantage.

   They are worth the time. Just think of it as one more dimension of your larger job search—another open door to your next position.

THE NEWSPAPER

Open a national daily, and you are flooded with job postings. While skilled jobs are posted daily, specialist jobs and senior positions come in a supplement once a week, for example, the *Times Accent* of the Times of India. Many companies provide 'walk-in interviews', giving the time and location of such interviews. Such job listings are safe and reliable and will address the specific organisation only. Send your resume by email as directed. Make sure that you have the right address and person to whom you should send your resume. Also, look for the last date for sending in your resume.

TRADE MAGAZINES

Trade magazines are those that target a specific industry. Some of them are sponsored by the industry association. For example, 'Advertising Age', 'Electronic News', 'Trade Art', etc. are specific to the advertising, electronic, or art industries. Such magazines advertise job openings specific to the industry. If you are educated, experienced, and trained for an industry, such magazines will save you time and help you focus on exactly what you want.

RECRUITMENT AGENCIES

These are the most popular these days. Many organisations approach recruitment agencies as a means of protecting their identity till the end. Organisations want to protect their identity for several reasons: they do not want their competition to know that they are recruiting; they want to protect themselves from recommendations of stakeholders whom they cannot refuse; they do not want their employees to know that certain positions are being filled; and they want to keep certain projects and positions secret. The recruitment agent then becomes the wonderful intermediary who will do the preliminary screening. They will provide several candidates for the organisation to choose from.

Most recruitment agents charge the organisation and not the candidate. They may charge you a nominal registration fee only. Smaller recruitment agents may charge the candidate as well. An advantage of going to a recruitment agent is that he or she knows of job openings that are not advertised. They will ask for your resume. Treat such agents as though they are the end organisation. They must be impressed with your credentials first before your resume is passed on. Their reputation is based on the quality of candidates they provide to the organisation.

Another benefit of a recruitment agent is that they prepare you for the interview. They give you tips on how to succeed with a particular organisation. They also have vast information on the organisation and can give you the dope you require for preparation to work out your strategies for the interview.

EMPLOYMENT EXCHANGES

Employment exchanges are usually sponsored by the state or federal government. They do have a large job listing base. Most of them, however, list positions at skilled levels in the public sector. Those with craft-level qualifications can benefit most from employment exchanges.

COLLEGE NOTICE BOARDS

Most universities and colleges list jobs on their 'Job Notice Boards'. These are ideal for undergrads and graduating students who are looking for part-time jobs or full-time jobs at the entry level into an organisation. Many universities and specialised colleges have their own placement cells. It is best to register with them, as they have contacts with industry and promote their university or college students for entry-level positions. The placement cell will also give you interview tips. Some placement cells invite the industry to come to campus and conduct their interviews, like the IIMs, IITs, and hotel management schools.

CRISIS! CAREERS AFTER 40

Here is something for you to sit on. In today's environment, organisations prefer youth and are quick to replace you once you reach 35–40 years old. They adopt this preference for several reasons: 1) organisations (especially service-oriented ones in the new service age) maintain long hours of work. Youth bring energy to cope with these long hours; 2) knowledge and skills get obsolete very quickly these days (e.g., the camera and cell phone industries bring new developments every six months). Youth bring in new knowledge learned in schools; 3) youth are more ambitious and are willing to take risks to outperform others. 4) Youth are more creative and less burdened with past practices. So when you hit 35, start thinking seriously about re-engineering yourself before the crisis of age hits you. Mature people with families are less flexible.

Think like a professional sportsperson. They are considered 'old' once they reach 35 years. Many re-engineer themselves to become sports commentators, coaches, sports journalists, TV sports anchors, etc. You must follow their principles. Before the layoff strikes, prepare yourself in advance.

The industry is also readjusting rapidly to survive. Uncomfortable words for jobseekers include "downsizing, acquisitions, mergers, closures, cutbacks, and layoffs." We hear of layoffs by even the most reputed companies because the dynamics of business have changed. The recent pandemic hit company sales all over. Companies were forced to get leaner and meaner to survive. No one wants to lose their job, especially with rising gas, utility, and cost-of-living prices. Just the mention of proposed company changes has made employees feel insecure. People rely on their incomes; therefore, identifying any hint of a layoff is critical to jobseeker survival. Facing unemployment can be daunting, but the true test is how you prepare for it with the time you're given.

Unlike days past, companies rarely announce an upcoming layoff unless the story is leaked and somehow makes the six o'clock news! There are several reasons for this. Market dynamics are sudden, and companies have to realign to those sudden changes, which can even include layoffs; employees'switch'off' when they hear of an impending change and may even sabotage such efforts; companies do not want their stocks to plummet in the share market with rumours of an impending disaster, etc.

WAYS TO TELL THAT YOU NEED TO LOOK FOR ANOTHER JOB:

It hurts to get axed, sacked, canned, or fired. It does nothing for your self-esteem, and it doesn't look great on your resume. You're always better off leaving your position on your own terms. But how can you tell when your job may be on the line? Here are some cues:

a. ***Company restructuring:***

   A management or executive-level restructuring, elimination of a second or third shift, and changes in inventory or production levels are all signs that something is going on. Ask co-workers, particularly those involved with inventory and clients, how things are going. Account managers, for example, will be the first to know when a large client won't be renewing a major contract or if sales have dropped significantly. An inventory and procurement professional will be the one to ask whether suppliers have stopped being delivered to due to late or non-payment issues.

b. ***News from the outside:***

Check the pulse of the local media. The web, newspapers, and business publications can offer a window into the financial health of your employer. Stories and articles covering missed contracts or severed business relationships should capture your interest. Keep in mind, negative indications don't mean you should react hastily. Companies always undergo changes—more so in today's market. Cutting the fat and shifting to lean operations is a necessity to staying profitable and continuing to grow in competitive markets. As companies are being transformed, retraining or cutting back on staff is sometimes unavoidable.

c. ***Your boss is finding too many faults:***

If you're being pulled up frequently by the boss, it means that he or she is making a case for your dismissal. They have made up their mind, and instead of honestly telling you about a layoff, they start finding faults in your work. It is a cue that it's time to start looking through the help-wanted classifieds.

d. ***When the boss is ignoring you:***

This is a dangerous signal. It means the boss has made up their mind already. No new assignments, instructions, or projects are coming your way. This is an indication that they are going to someone else or keeping it pending for a new incumbent. You may even find that you are excluded from meetings, and important communication is not coming your way.

e. ***Your co-workers start avoiding you:***

Office gossip spreads like wildfire, and all too often, everybody knows before you do. Sure, it's unprofessional, but it happens all the time. You will notice surreptitious glimpses or that conversations suddenly stop when you approach them. So, if your workplace friends start to shun you, ask people if they've heard anything. A good friend will tell you. A lousy friend will run screaming from the room! Either way, it's time to move on.

f. ***The HR director has your file on his table:***

You may wonder why, all of a sudden, the people in HR have pulled out your file. Be suspicious.

g. ***You read a job ad for your position:***

This happens very often. Employers like continuity in a job position and seek replacements before they break the news to you. If you happen to run across your job description in the classifieds, in an ad placed by your company, keep looking. You're probably in the market for a new job – which was why you were reading the help-wanted section in the first place.

h. ***You've been frequently absent due to domestic obligations:***

Your employer does not like this. In the fast-paced workplace, supervisors want 'warm bodies' to complete the daily tasks. Your absence can be very annoying. Employers expect you to be at work, and when you aren't, productivity falls, and someone has to cover for you. Good employees go to work and do their jobs. Those who take excessive leave are guaranteed to be on the block.

i. ***A bunch of new trainees are hired from local colleges:***

This could mean that the company has plans to infuse new blood into the organisation. They are cheaper than you at 40 years and are poised to replace you and all others like you.

ACTION PLAN

Getting sacked rarely comes as a complete surprise. There are usually signs that things aren't right at work – signs that you may choose to ignore but shouldn't. Keep your eyes and ears open for signs of trouble. A change in company ownership, a new supervisor, a new set of company procedures, a drop in sales, etc. Dramatic changes can often lead to layoffs, belt-tightening, and lots of 'Good Luck' parties.

Let's say the above signs are present in your situation. Immediately shift into survival mode, especially if the layoff is rumoured to happen within hours or days. Here are a few tips to re-engineer yourself:

Build on What You Know

You have experience, and that's valuable. To walk away from 15 years in marketing to become a goat herder is not a good career move. Build on what you know.

Examples:

An auto engineer picks up a temporary teaching certificate after a three-month crash course in principles of education and becomes a high school CAD instructor. It doesn't pay as much, but the intangible rewards more than offset the smaller paycheck.

A real estate agent, tired of the late-night phone calls and 60-hour work weeks, starts flipping properties on the side. She knows the market, the inspectors, the contractors, the lenders – she's plugged into the local real estate grid from the top down. So, she takes what she knows (of immense value) and starts her own property management company, buying, selling, and renting properties.

A CPA becomes Director of Development for a local non-profit organisation. A paediatric nurse takes the helm at a drop-off kid care franchise.

A Food and Beverage Manager opens his own restaurant. Another one acts as a consultant to smaller restaurant entrepreneurs.

You get the idea? Build on what you've got.

Make a Critical Self-Assessment

Sit down with a nice cup of coffee and make a list of your professional knowledge, skills, and competencies that could be leveraged in a new career. You'll be surprised at the extent of your skill set.

Your list should include proficiency using computer software programmes (these are transportable skills required in almost every job), special training, and knowledge acquired on the job.

Now, here's where the coffee comes in. Make a second list of your professional weaknesses. Make a third list of your personal qualities.

Maybe it may open new doors. Sometimes we have talents and attitudes that were kept locked throughout your career so far. You need to open those doors and do something you like. I took authorship after 30 years in corporate life. I went to a writing course. It was marvellous. Maybe it is time to go back to school and do a short-term course yourself.

Update your Resume:

When did you last update your resume? Do so now and start scanning for potential employers. Remember, I mentioned above about reading newspapers and business publications? Those same publications can be a huge asset to you while you're job searching because they also tell you what companies are expanding, landing the big contracts, and expecting to see growth. Look at industries (possibly outside your current one) that aren't facing job losses because you don't want to jump from one sinking ship to another.

Go Back to School:

Continuous education is the byword of today's professionals. Unless you keep up to date, you are not going to survive in the market that is changing each day. One of the reasons for getting laid off is your obsolete knowledge and skills. Younger generations come out of college with the latest knowledge and are therefore preferred. Adult education, the local community college, technical schools, four-year universities, workshops, and seminars are all great places to develop new skills and update old ones. Get the certificate, licence, degree, or credentials you need to start down your new career path. I have known defence personnel who studied short courses in hotel management to find jobs as security officers and administration managers in hotels. Air Force Pilots got commercial licences to fly commercial jets.

Study the Job Market:

Check out what's hot and what's not. Well, the IT sector seems to be hot again. There's unprecedented demand for Back Processing Offices (BPOs) and trainers at all levels.

Go through the classifieds to see what's hot in your region. Or maybe you're willing to relocate. That'll expand your options! Many start-up companies value experience. They can get you on board as an adviser, consultant, retainer, etc.

Back-door Entry:

You have another option if you are asked to leave. You could negotiate being re-hired as a retainer by the same company. A retainer works on a contract basis, perhaps at a lower pay. organisations look at such methods to cut payroll costs. A retainer does not attract the benefits and superannuation costs to burden the company. A company values your knowledge of the company's systems, practices, and processes and prefers an old experienced hand than having to train someone new.

Another good method of associating with your company is to become a supplier or contractor to it. Many organisations believe in outsourcing services as a viable strategy. The horticulturist of a hotel was laid off and was hired as a contractor to maintain the gardens of the property. The continuity of the horticulture programme was maintained. An engineer in a motor company became the supplier of spark plugs to the factory. He knew exactly the needs and standards of the manufacturer and was able to source cheaper spark plugs of quality. A Director of Engineering became the technical trainer of the company. A Human Resources Manager started her own recruitment firm supplying human resources to her old company.

Leverage your connections with the organisation to serve it in other ways than straight employment. Your experience counts.

Career Counselling

If it's offered, take it. You've been laid off, but the company still cares enough to help you find a new job. Take advantage. It's free, and it may help you land your next job two months faster. Alternatively, seek the help of a professional career counsellor if you are stuck. Remember, these are new times, and a professional career counsellor can help you align yourself with the new trends using your present talents. They will also advise you about other courses you can take to make you more eligible in the market.

References:

References are a must. They will stand in good stead in your next career. Don't stop with your immediate supervisor. Get letters of reference from higher-ups too. The Human Resources department is authorised to give official references, but there's no harm in getting ones from other well-wishers in the organisation.

Letters from clients and customers also look good in an employment package, so don't be shy about calling a few of your best customers and asking for a letter of recommendation. They are very impressive to a future employer.

Leave on a Good Note:

You will never know when you will need the support of your organisation in your future career. They may even call you back when circumstances change. Your associates could be good network points to get you through many doors.

Leave on the best terms possible. Leave with a lot of handshakes, smiles, and best wishes all around.

The absolute worst thing you can do is quit without a plan of action. That's like walking a tightrope without a net. If at all possible, give your notice, clean out your desk, and move on to the rest of your life, starting first thing Monday morning.

The key is to find a job – any job – to keep the creditors at bay. Build on your skill set by designing a resume, cover letter, and thank-you letter that demonstrate how your skills translate to this new position, business, or industry.

Three

Creating a Hotshot Resume

I feel compelled to write about a properly presented resume. In my experience as a recruiter, several resumes found their way to the delete dustbin because of the improper and shabby way they were presented. Such resumes were just not appealing enough to motivate me to read them. I do not want this to happen to you. Some resumes I received left a positive impression on me and spurred me to anxiously want to meet them. This chapter will deal with how to make winning resumes that are informative and appealing. But first, let us understand what a resume is.

WHAT IS A RESUME?

A resume is you. It is a documented profile of you, the candidate, and reflects your personality. It can either destroy or augment your chances of being called for an interview. A resume (French term), is also called a Curriculum Vitae (Latin term) or Bio-Data (English term). The term most understood in your location must be used. The resume is your first introduction to the recruiters and explains your education, experience, achievements, and character. It is your calling card which is viewed well before a physical meeting with the interviewers. It, therefore, must evoke enough interest to the selector to shortlist it for an interview. Your objective in the first instance is to present the best document to get a call.

Resumes are formal *legal documents*. Information presented must be *authentic*. These can be verified, and good organisations do verify them through formal and informal references. organisations ask for documentary proof of qualifications, experience, and date of birth. A few candidates lose their jobs because of unsupported documents. Bluffing through is a minefield, and candidates are summarily dropped or dismissed when they are found out providing false misinformation and claims.

PURPOSE OF A RESUME

The primary purpose of a resume is to secure an interview. The resume is your "sales tool" and provides you with an opportunity to market your strengths and accomplishments to prospective employers. You will want to communicate your skills, education, experience, and interests to a potential employer. This information will assist the employer in assessing your ability to do the work. There is no one right resume; however, a concise, well-written, easy to read resume will attract attention and will increase your chances of being invited to an interview.

Preparing a Resume (See sample resume at the end of the chapter)

You can make a meal in 10 minutes. You can have the oil in your car changed in 10 minutes. You can do a lot of things in 10 minutes, but writing a resume isn't one of them. Not if you are serious about finding a good job. Anything good takes time to polish. You have to make your resume distinctive from others to get noticed. Many candidates use stereotyped methods as though they were cut from a template. You want your resume to sizzle and sell.

Creating the right resume is an art. It's a skill you can learn, but creativity is an important aspect of the perfect resume, and that's where the art part starts.

If you are in doubt, go to a professional resume writer. If you went to one, they would take time to get to know you and your job search objectives. They will ask for extensive details about your work activities, looking for that little 'hook' that will set you apart from the competitors. They would spotlight your strongest attributes as a job candidate. Professional resume writers are also current on employment trends, using current buzzwords that sizzle to make you look really professional.

What Does a Personalised Resume Do For You?

- Your resume is not a string of dates, places, and job duties. It is a **sales tool** that excites a recruiter.
- A professionally prepared resume is **perfect**. No typos, no misspellings, and no slang. A resume with a gross spelling error is doomed to the delete dustbin! It shows your lack of an eye for detail.
- A well-packaged resume and cover letter say a great deal about your **professionalism**. It shows the employer that you know the rules of the business or commercial world.
- Isn't your professional future **worth the effort** of crafting a good resume?

Destination Dustbin - Bad Resumes

Those who do not give enough importance to this vital document show the following pitfalls that force me to reject them:

1. It has spelling errors.
2. It is a photocopy (shows that the resume is being sent to several places).
3. There is no covering letter.
4. Undated covering letter.
5. Covering letter not addressed to a specific person.
6. The information is incomplete.
7. It does not give the formal name.
8. It does not have an address.
9. It does not give a contact number.
10. It does not have a photograph.
11. The candidate has not dressed for the photograph.
12. Candidates in the photograph do not smile. They are rather grim mug shots (Like convicts!).

13. Information is not presented in the correct preferable sequence.
14. The qualifications and experience do not match the profile of the job (shows that the candidate has applied blindly).

Basic Guidelines for a Good Resume

- You must tell the truth.
- It is your job to sell yourself.
- A resume is about your future, not your past.
- Put information in order of interest to your reader.

You must tell the **truth** in your resume. That's not negotiable. It is simply unethical to invent any part of your background. Ensure that you can support your information with proof. Employers will verify the basic facts on any resume, especially your title, dates of employment, prior salary history, and your qualifications. If you do land yourself a job based on lies, there is no job security. Most employers will dismiss employees, even years later, if they are discovered to have lied on their applications. Your resume is a legal document that becomes part of your permanent personnel file. Being creative and persuasive does not mean creating a piece of fiction.

Sell yourself. The resume is no place for modesty. Employers expect you to showcase your skills, competencies, talents, traits, and experiences relative to their needs. You are doing them a favourif you put your best foot forward because they are looking at your resume specifically to discover your talents and abilities. While selling yourself, always focus on those attributes the employer needs. Perhaps your reference letters from school, college, and work will provide you with the right words. Ask your best friend or family member to fill you in on what they perceive as your strengths. We are often unaware of them.

A good resume is focused on your **future**. It will communicate your career objectives, aspirations, and ambitions. The information should be organised in the order of interest to your reader. It should be customised for each job application, whether it is an internship or a job opportunity. The job you are applying for must align with your career goals. Therefore, a resume should be designed to help create the future you want, not just report your past. This is why we start working on your resume not by compiling information from your past but by imagining your future.

Interest the reader. Many resumes are long-winded and boring. It is an effort to go through them because they are not concise and to the point. They become a history sheet. Capture the reader's interest with some key phrases that will make him or her want to continue reading. Consider your employer and customise your resume for them. Research the industry that you want to work for and assess their needs, then create a resume that highlights how you can contribute to them. emphasise the skills that relate most to the position you are applying for, highlighting any growth in your responsibilities. An ideal resume should have a maximum of two pages. If they want a snapshot resume, it should be one page only.

1. Use action words such as "supervised," "directed," "developed," "organised," and "planned" to describe what you are capable of doing.
2. Highlight qualities or skills at which you excel or that are unique to you.
3. Place the most relevant information near the top of your resume and highlight the skills that relate to the type of work you are seeking.
4. Focus on what you can do for the company/organisation with reference to your past achievements.
5. Use short, specific, descriptive statements to illustrate that your skills, experience, and education match the employer's requirements.
6. Be truthful about your accomplishments – do not undersell yourself, but do not exaggerate either – this could come back to haunt you in the interview.
7. Include your name, telephone number, complete home and e-mail addresses.
8. Include your other interests.

Resume Format – General Guidelines

The following guidelines follow typical resume format standards. These are general resume format rules:

* Use a font size of 10 or 12.
* Make it perfectly typed with about a 1-inch margin.
* Use only one font (preferably Times New Roman, Arial, Tahoma, or Verdana). You may vary the size for emphasis, if necessary.
* Use bold print for emphasis, but do not use too many different styles.
* Avoid all-capital letters and italics as they are difficult to read.
* Describe training, skills, and accomplishments in phrases rather than sentences.
* Use action verbs to encourage reader interest and response.

Good resumes follow a proper sequence of information that is generally accepted. You must keep in mind that the selector is a busy person and is inundated with several applications and will need to get the right information immediately from the resume to raise interest to carry on further. Here is a suggested sequence of information:

* **Title (Resume)**
* **Name, Address, and Contact Number**
* **Career Objective, Aspiration, Ambition**
* **Special Skills and Competencies for the Job**
* **Past Achievements that Relate to the New Job**
* **Educational Qualifications**
* **Special Courses Attended**
* **Experience**
* **Hobbies and Interests**
* **Personal Information**

- **References**
- **Signature**

Let us look at each in detail:

Title: This refers to the heading of the document. It must be titled as 'Resume,' 'Bio-data,' or 'Curriculum Vitae.' Use the term used by the organisation when they advertised for the position. Apparently, it is the term that they are using and understand at their workplace.

Name, Address, and Contact Numbers: The name must be in the sequence of first name, middle name, and surname. There are certain cultures where the village or father's name is given, like in the state of Kerala, India. Since the names are adaptations to the local dialects, some candidates may use initials like C.V. George. Whatever the style used, it must correspond exactly to the way it is presented in the passport, driving licence, or school leaving certificate. These are documents accepted universally to authenticate names. Remember that certain statutory funds like the provident fund, pension, government gratuity fund, or social insurance are redeemable by showing documentary evidence of names. Therefore, your name as reflected in the resume will be logged as the official name in the company records for contributions to such funds.

Address: The e-mail address must be reliable over a long period of time for immediate and long-term contact. The company will use the e-mail address mentioned in the resume for correspondence, especially for calling you for an interview; rejection letters; correspondence during service; legal notices; cheques of statutory funds which arrive long after a candidate has left the service.

Contact Numbers: This is vital for all immediate contact concerning the interview and subsequent official conversation. The most valuable contact number these days is the mobile number. However the mobile number can be switched off or where networks do not work. It is therefore important to give alternate numbers like the residence land-line number. It is important to keep the mobile number 'on' to be contacted at any time. It must be kept open but in silent if you are in cinema halls or areas that prohibit mobile numbers.

Career Objective: Selectors these days are keen to know the reason for your applying for a job. This gives them the indication as to your motivation. Think this through carefully as it could enhance your chances or destroy it for selection. Selectors want serious applicants and are keen to match your objective to their objectives of employment. Remember that the interviewer may probe the reason for your applying at the time of interview, so the reason stated must be defendable. Some of the reasons for wanting to apply are:

- Entry into the workplace after your education
- Change of job for a position that matches your skill set, more appropriately
- Change of job for advancement
- Move to an organisation that offers better career prospects
- Move to a larger organisation
- Move to an organisation that offers individual growth
- Move to an organisation that recognises good talent
- Moving into a state or city for personal reasons

While the reasons above are legitimate reasons some of them can be double edge swords too. For example a change of job for advancement gives the fear to the interviewer that that you will leave them if get a better offer elsewhere while in service with them. The interviewer will check your employment record and see the frequency with which you changed jobs. Too many changes will indicate that you are chasing money alone. While this is a valid reason for change, after all everyone wants to improve their lot, organisations are wary of job hoppers.

Here are some typical examples of career objectives:

"To seek employment at the entry level that matches my qualifications and aspirations."

"To join an organisation that will utilise my education and experience to mutual benefit."

"To join an organisation where we can grow together using my skill sets and experience."

"I am seeking employment as I believe that my profile best suits the job advertised."

"To grow in the energy sector as it is my chosen field."

"To join a growing organisation that will help me grow with it."

Special Skills and Competencies: First, let us understand what is meant by 'skills' and 'competencies.' *Skills* are abilities to execute certain specific tasks for a definite purpose. A machinist must have the skill to operate a lathe machine. An accountant must have bookkeeping skills to fulfil the job. *Competencies* are behaviours essential to a job. Both the machinist and accountant must be perfectionists. Any deviation in their jobs can have serious impacts on their work. An air hostess loves to serve people, a salesman loves to communicate with people, a project technician likes to work in a team. Let us look at some more examples of both:

Skills

Technical (handling machines, acting, modelling, accounting, business, etc)

Computer

Communication

Analytical

Customer Service

Management

People

Negotiation

Selling

Competencies

Teamwork

Leadership

Coordination

Customer orientation

Grooming and hygiene

Courtesy and manners

Result-oriented

Disciplined

Critical Thinking

To understand the difference between the two we can explain this in another way. A counter salesperson must have the skill to sell a product. This is acquired through training and experience. This same salesperson cannot sell successfully if s/he does not have the competency of courtesy and manners. One is an ability to perform and the other is behaviour while performing.

Achievements: This showcases the achievements of the past that shows promise of the future. This gives the selector a snapshot of what honours you have acquired in your past jobs. Selectors like to hire those who are result oriented. The achievements must mention the quantity, time and place of the performance. Here are some good examples of achievements:

- Increased sales by 20% in the year 2006 at Goodwin Park Ltd.
- Achieved a labour cost saving of 40% in 2005 at Hyundai Factory.
- Got the "Employee of the Year" recognition for three consecutive years since 2001 at Pullman Hops LLC.
- Successfully trained 20 customer service executives who achieved a 20% increase in sales at Hero Honda in the year 1999.

Examples of Bad Achievement Statements:

- Increased sales.
- Saved labour costs.
- Got recognition for performance.
- Trained 20 customer service executives.

What if you do not have any achievements? This is a serious matter, and you must look at yourself and your performance. Someone with achievements is likely to score above you at the time of selection. Do not be surprised if you are not shortlisted. But this is the gloomy side of things. On the positive side, everyone has achieved something at work or at school, which you took for granted. It is just that you have not thought about it. You may have been a sports captain in school or a prefect or won a declamation contest. This example shows you to be a leader and a good communicator. Search for your achievements and list them down. At work, you may have at least achieved the targets set for you in a year. Good. Then list this achievement as:

"Achieved targets throughout my working career, leading to an above-average performance rating."

"I achieved a zero percent absentee rate during my career."

Wow! In the above examples, I as a recruiter can expect you to achieve the targets set for you with a zero absentee record. I like such workers who show commitment and achieve results.

Academic Qualifications: These must be presented with the most recent first. Those with good qualifications would like to showcase them prominently to get the edge over other candidates. Educational qualifications can be presented in two ways: the running style or through a table, as follows:

Running Style:

1985-1987 Masters in Business Administration from the Faculty of Management Studies, Delhi University

!982-1985 Bachelor of Commerce from Sri Ram College of Commerce, Delhi University High School (Class XII) from Modern School, New Delhi

1978-1981 Junior High (Class X) from Modern School, New Delhi

Table Style:

From	To	Educational Institution	Qualification	Rating
1985	1987	Faculty of Management Studies, Delhi University	Masters in Business Administration	B
1982	1985	Sri Ram College of Commerce, Delhi University	Bachelor of Commerce	92%
1981	1982	Modern School, New Delhi	High School (Class XII)	95%
1978	1981	Modern School, New Delhi	Junior High School (Class X)	95%

You may ask, ***"What if I did not study in well-known institutions?"*** Be proud of where you studied. I appreciated those candidates who were proud of their school and college, irrespective of whether it was well-known or not. I felt that they would show the same fierce loyalty and pride in my organisation. Never undermine your institution and prepare to highlight all the good qualities you imbibed from it. Flaunt it during the interview.

Another pertinent question you may ask is, ***"What if I did not get good marks in school or college?"*** Do not mention your grades on the resume. Let the interviewer inquire about it during the interview. You can respond by saying, *"I am more of a hands-on person than an academic."* I have found in my experience that those who are not academically inclined are not necessarily poor performers. As a matter of fact, such candidates went that extra mile to prove to themselves that they were just as good as others. And they were, if not better. Your scholastic marks may have affected your admission to prestigious colleges, but what matters now is 'you' and how you have shaped up. Your intrinsic qualities, backed by your achievements at work, must override your average marks and should be highlighted. That is what matters at the moment. You may consider mentioning your educational qualifications after your work experience if that is more impressive.

Special Courses Attended: These are important technical courses to help you specialise in specific skills. They show the interviewer your interest in continuous education and your commitment to staying updated. Technical courses are short-term, ranging from 3 days to less than a year. Most of them end with a certificate of proficiency, participation, or achievement. These courses can also be presented in a running style or in the form of a table.

Running Style:

Nov' 1983 — 2- weeks programme on Microsoft Office Applications by Aptech Ltd, New Delhi

Sep' 1989 — 3-day 'Train the Trainer' programme by the Indian Society for Training & Development, Mumbai

Table Style:

Date	Duration	Institution	Name of Programme	Certification
Nov' 1983	2-weeks	Aptech Ltd. New Delhi	Microsoft Applications	Certificate of Proficiency
Sep' 1989	3 days	Indian Society of Training & Development, Mumbai	Train-the-Trainer	Certificate of Achievement

Experience: Your experience is perhaps the most important part of your resume when seeking a job. Obviously, selectors try to match the experience to the job profile of the position. Experience concerns involve two things: 1) Quality of experience and 2) Duration of experience (number of years). Your experience should meet the expectations of the organisation. Most organisations mention these two concerns in the job advertisement itself. Some candidates disregard these expectations and apply anyway. It is a waste of time for both you and the selector. Ensure that your experience aligns with what they want.

Your experience can be presented in a running style or in a table as well. It should commence with the most recent experience.

Running Style:

1. **XYZ Co. Ltd.** **Marketing Supervisor** **July 2000 till date**

Responsibilities:

* Led a team of six salespersons who consistently exceeded sales targets.
* Coached six team members in negotiating skills, resulting in increased order volume.
* Coordinated with the warehouse to ensure timely supply of goods, maintaining a record of zero supply delays.
* Managed relationships with transporters to achieve on-time delivery and keep transportation costs within budget.
* Monitored production schedules to ensure timely delivery.
* Provided exceptional customer service, earning several commendation letters from clients.
* Prepared accurate invoices for goods with a zero percent recovery factor.
* Successfully accounted for goods sold and consistently met sales targets.

Achievements:

* Expanded the market segment by 20%.
* Achieved a 10% increase in sales compared to the previous year.
* Maintained a track record of delivering orders on time.

2. **ABC company** **Sr. Salesman** **Jan' 1992 – Jul' 2000**

Responsibilities:

* Developed sales leads throughout South Asia.
* Ascertained sales requirements and negotiated prices.
* Sourced pipe manufacturers.

* Evaluated pipe manufacturers for our needs.
* Recommended suitable manufacturers to the Sales Manager for short-term and long-term orders.
* Monitored and followed up on manufacturers' production schedules.
* Coordinated with shipping and transportation for ex-factory delivery.
* Managed and completed all sales documentation.

Achievements:

* Increased sources of supply by 12%.
* Expanded sales leads by 30%.

Table Style:

Sr. No.	Period From	Period to	Name of Organisation	Designation	Brief Responsibilities
1.	Jul' 2000	Till date	XYZ Co. Ltd	Marketing Supervisor	* Led a team of six sales persons to achieve sales targets * Coaching team members * Coordination with warehouse for supply of goods * Coordination with shipping and transportation of goods * Customer Service and handling complaints * Raising invoices for goods * Accounting for goods sold
2.	Jan' 1992	Jul' 2000	ABC Co. Ltd.	Senior Salesman	* Develop sales leads throughout South Asia * Ascertain sales requirements and negotiate prices * Source pipe manufacturers * Evaluate pipe manufacturers for our needs * Recommend to Sales Manager such manufacturers for short-term and long-term orders. * Follow-up on manufacturers production schedules * Coordinate with shipping and transportation for ex-factory delivery * Complete all sales documentation

Interviewer's Point of View:

When reading the example given above, the interviewer will likely deduce the following about you and your experience:

- You have experience in the oil piping industry (as you applied to this specific industry).
- You possess sales and marketing expertise.
- You demonstrate leadership skills.
- You excel in coaching and mentoring others.
- You are proficient in sales accounting and documentation.
- You exhibit strong coordination and follow-up abilities.
- You are results-oriented and have a track record of achieving goals.
- You contribute to business growth.
- You value punctuality and time management.
- You have a stable employment history and are not a frequent job changer.

Hobbies and Interests: Let's differentiate between hobbies, interests, and pastimes. **Hobbies** are activities outside of work in which you have extensive knowledge, skills, and proficiency. Examples include aero modelling, philately (stamp collection), numismatics (coin collection), sculpture, painting, music, gardening, and more. **Interests** are subjects or areas you have knowledge about but may not actively participate in or be highly proficient at. For instance, you might have an interest in cricket, airplanes, cars, politics, etc., without active involvement. It's essential to list a few hobbies or even just one if you possess in-depth knowledge.

Pastimes, on the other hand, are passive leisure activities like watching television, eating, window shopping, reading, listening to music, etc. While pastimes are rarely mentioned in resumes, some individuals, particularly the younger generation, might take pride in highlighting them, although this is generally discouraged.

This segment of the resume is especially important for those starting their careers in entry-level jobs. Since there is no experience to write about, the interviewer will want to learn about your character through your hobbies and interests. When presenting them on the resume, it is better to list achievements rather than activities. For example:

Activity: **I play cricket**

Achievement: Represented school and college in cricket.

Interviewer's Point of View

Hobbies and interests reveal the following:

- Whether you are creative or logical
- Whether you are active or passive
- Whether you are curious or cursory
- Whether you are achievement-oriented or an 'also-ran'
- Whether you are a leader or a follower
- Whether you are committed or fickle

Therefore, any form of art is considered creative. An interest in crosswords, chess, or aero modelling shows you are logical. Participation in any form of outdoor sport shows you are active, whereas origami, board games, or reading shows you are passive. Certificates of achievement indicate that you have attained some level of performance, whereas certificates of participation indicate that you were part of the crowd. Holding positions such as captain, prefect, supervisor, chairman, team leader, etc., demonstrates leadership, whereas being a member of a team activity portrays you as a good follower.

Personal: Personal information may include the following:

- Date of birth
- Whether in possession of a passport (necessary for international assignments)
- Whether in possession of a driving licence (necessary for outdoor jobs)

- Whether in possession of own car (some outdoor jobs may insist on this and they may provide a petrol allowance)

There are some states that believe in equal opportunities and cannot ask for the following information:

- Marital status
- Religion
- Caste or tribe (in India, this may be necessary to mention to be considered for quotas given to scheduled castes and tribes, referred to as SC/ST)
- Race or colour
- Gender orientation

References: There are two types of references:

a. Character reference

b. Work reference

Character Reference: An organisation would like to ensure that when they select you, they are choosing a law-abiding, honest, and reliable person. Your antecedents are therefore important to the organisation. The only tool available to the organisation is the reference of responsible individuals who can vouch for you.

Your resume should have at least three referees who are not relatives. The higher the status of the referee, the more credibility you will have. To obtain these references, you must seek their permission first. The references quoted must provide full names, addresses, and telephone numbers. Professional organisations will contact these referees by phone or in writing to obtain independent references about you. Make sure you identify the right people who will provide positive accounts about you.

Work Reference: Another kind of reference is one provided by a previous employer. Good professionals will always seek reference letters from their former employers. Such letters not only confirm the duration of your employment with them but also testify to your conduct and performance. Some organisations may be displeased about your departure and will provide only a letter confirming the duration of your employment with them. This is better than nothing. File these reference letters carefully, as they may be requested during interviews.

Signature: Nowadays, resumes are typically sent via email. In such cases, the applicant can send an unsigned resume but will need to provide a signed hard copy during the interview.

Photograph: A resume is considered complete with a photograph. When taking the photograph, ensure that you appear cheerful with a smile. Additionally, dress formally with a jacket and tie (for men) or a jacket and conservative blouse (for women). Please, remember to smile! Many passport photographs resemble those taken of convicts. Men should ensure they are clean-shaven, and women should have their hair neatly styled.

APPLICATION FORM:

Many organisations provide their own application forms, which are printed formats with relevant questions and spaces for you to fill in. Organisations request this information to obtain the specific details they require.

Filling out the Application Form:

- Ensure that all columns and spaces are completed. Use "N.A." (not applicable) for sections not relevant to you.
- Thoroughly review all columns before providing any information. If you find any questions or columns unclear, seek clarification from the organisation via phone.
- Carefully specify the position you are applying for.
- Include a good passport-sized photograph, following the guidelines mentioned earlier.
- Ensure that all supporting documents are properly scanned and enclosed with the application form.
- Take a photo of the completed application form to have a record to support the information during the interview. This photo also serves as proof of submission in case the form is misplaced by the organisation.

Final Check

Once you've composed your resume, take the time to review it meticulously for any mistakes and to refine your writing style.

- Check for errors! Have someone proofread your resume to ensure correct spelling, grammar, and punctuation.
- Avoid using "I" or "me" in your descriptions.
- Maintain a consistent format and use the same grammatical tense throughout your resume.
- Refrain from using "jargon" or abbreviations.
- Employ a variety of words to describe yourself (e.g. do not use "excellent" or "very" in every other statement).
- Diversify the structure of your statements.

Cover Letters

Remember the golden rule: **a resume must be accompanied by a covering letter.** Composing a cover letter may initially appear challenging, but with a few tips, you'll become proficient at crafting letters to send with your resume.

Your cover letter should complement, not duplicate, your resume. Its purpose is to interpret the data-oriented, factual resume and add a personal touch. A cover letter often serves as your earliest written contact with a potential employer, establishing a critical first impression.

Purpose of a Cover Letter

The purpose of a cover letter is to provide a brief introduction of both you and your resume in response to an advertised position or in anticipation of a possible opening. A well-crafted cover letter will effectively highlight your strengths and connect your abilities directly to the employer's needs, generating enough interest to secure an interview. The following are some helpful hints to keep in mind as you write.

Types of Cover Letters

There are three general types of cover letters:

- The application letter, which responds to a known job opening.
- The prospecting letter, which inquires about possible positions.
- The networking letter, which requests information and assistance in your job search.
- Your cover letter should be tailored specifically for each of the purposes outlined above, as well as for each position you seek.

Application Letter

Here are some tips:

- Your cover letter must be tailored to the specific job position.
- You should possess the qualifications required for the position.
- analyse the advertisement carefully.
- List the job criteria, then match your skills to them (See examples below).
- Research the organisation.

There are two styles for matching your skills to the job criteria: the paragraph style and the list style. Let's see the examples given below:

Job Advertisement:

BOX-OFFICE MANAGER: Conduct, oversee subscription and ticket sales for events. Generate and maintain reports, perform accounting activities related to box-office revenue, oversee operations. The position requires customer service skills and accounting experience.

Cover Letter Example 1: Paragraph Style

In my role as Box Office Assistant for the Light Opera Company, I was responsible for customer service, ticketing patrons, and generating and maintaining box office reports. Additionally, I meticulously managed records and accounting reports for all box office transactions.

Cover Letter Example 2: List Style

Box Office Manager Requirements:

- Conduct and oversee subscription and ticket sales for events
- Generate and maintain reports, and perform accounting activities
- Possess customer service skills and accounting experience

As you can observe, the candidate has effectively aligned their skills with the job criteria. This approach increases the likelihood of passing the initial screening because it directly addresses the job advertisement and explains why they are qualified for the position. **Do not apply if your skills, qualifications and experience do not match.**

COVER LETTER TEMPLATE

The following cover letter template outlines the essential information you should include in the cover letter that accompanies your resume. Utilise this template as a framework to create customised cover letters tailored for specific employers.

Your Name	
Your Address	
Your City, State, Zip Code	contact information
Your Phone Number	
Your Email Address	
Date	
Name	
Title	
Company	employer contact information
Address	
City, State, Zip Code	
Dear Mr./Ms last name	salutation

Subject.............	job position advertised
Body of the letter	
xxxxxxxxxxxxx	first paragraph
xxxxxxxxxxxxx	middle paragraph
xxxxxxxxxxx	concluding paragraph
Yours sincerely,	complimentary close
Signature	Your name and title

Contact Information

The first section of your cover letter should include information on how the employer can contact you. Make sure that the information is reliable and correct. Your career depends on it.

Employer Contact Information

The employer's contact information must be accurate. Normally, the job advertisement gives the right address. Make sure that you have the right zip code. In website job postings, the address is obtained by clicking 'contact us'.

Salutation

The standard salutation is "Dear Mr. or Mrs...." If you want to be different from the rest, find out the name of the advertiser. This can be obtained by simply calling the office and asking for it from the receptionist or the HR Department. Make sure you get the spelling right. Nothing is more insulting to a person than his name being spelled wrongly. A person's name is the most precious thing he or she has. Using the name becomes personal, and the reader will be impressed that you took the trouble to find out his or her name. Use the surname only. This is a formal correspondence, and only people who are known personally to the writer can accept the first name. I suggest that you use the surname, even if you know the person. The letter may pass through several hands in the organisation and we do not want to show familiarity.

Subject

The subject is the job position. An organisation gets several letters in a day. Your letter's subject immediately identifies the purpose of the letter. This is appreciated to segregate the letter from the rest of the correspondence received. Some ways you can write the subject are: 'Box-Office Manager', 'Job Announcement for Box-Office Manager', 'Vacancy for Box-Office Manager'.

Body of the Cover Letter

The body of your cover letter lets the employer know what position you are applying for, why the employer should select you for an interview, and how you will follow up.

First Paragraph:

The first paragraph of your letter should include information on why you are writing. Mention the position you are applying for. Mention that you are qualified for the position. Be clear and concise regarding your request.

- *Name the job for which you are applying and tell how you learned about it.*
- *State that you are qualified to do the job based on your background (give the employer a sense of your confidence in your own abilities).*
- *State that you are very interested in the job or the organisation and indicate a specific or unique reason why this job or organisation appeals to you, which in turn shows that you have done some research (keep this brief).*

It would read something like this:

"I am applying for the position of box office manager advertised in the Times of India on July 27th... I seem to have the requisite qualifications and experience for the position. I am looking to enhance my professional growth and find that your organisation is ideally suited to my career aspirations as well as the chance to use my skills to contribute to your organisation's prosperity".

Middle Paragraphs:

The next section of your cover letter should describe what you have to offer the employer. Convince the reader that they should grant the interview or appointment you requested in the first paragraph. Make strong connections between your abilities and their needs. Mention specifically how your skills and experience match the job you are applying for. Remember, you are interpreting your resume, not repeating it. Try to support each statement you make with a piece of evidence. Use several shorter paragraphs or bullets rather than one large block of text. Use the matching text exercise you did earlier.

- Determine what you are going to discuss in terms of your education, work experience, skills, interests, personality, and beliefs (focus on the ones that address the job's most important requirements).
- Subdivide the body into sections. One possibility is that the first paragraph describes what you have to offer, and the second describes your interest in and knowledge about the organisation
- State the skills and strengths you will bring to the job (address all those asked for in the job advertisement) and include examples or descriptions of how you have acquired and demonstrated each skill or strength.
- Explain how the skills and strengths you mention would be useful in the new position.
- When including an example of your abilities, be specific to allow the employer to visualise what you have done and can do (quantify: how long did you do it, how much responsibility you have, what techniques did you use, and why were they useful?)

"I am a graduate of the arts with five years of experience in the theatre business. In my present position as Box Office Assistant for the Light Opera Company, I am responsible for customer service, ticketing patrons, and generating and maintaining box office reports. In addition, I maintained records and accounting reports for all box office transactions. I have learned that your progressive organisation is looking for someone with my skills and aspirations. I have been a team leader for one year with responsibilities to motivate and train counter salespersons". Or "I am a team person who is detailed and has exceptional customer skills. I have good oral and written communication skills."

Final Paragraph:

Conclude your cover letter by thanking the employer for considering you for the position. Enclose your. If your body section is more than one paragraph, restate that you are qualified to do the job, but make this sentence different from the one in your opening paragraph.

- Thank the employer for taking the time to consider your application.
- State that you would like to meet in person or via digital media to further discuss the job and your qualifications, or that you hope to hear from them soon.
- If your application was unsolicited, tell the employer that you will be contacting them in a few days to discuss your application and to possibly set up an interview.
- You may also want to tell the employer where and when you can be contacted if they require further information (optional).

It will read like this:

"I thank you for your consideration and look forward to an interview".

Complimentary Close:

Respectfully yours,

Signature:

Name and title for your computer submission.

You will notice that the letter is concise, to the point, and targeted at the job. Remember that the interviewer has little time and welcomes letters that give the message in a brief yet effective manner.

Prospecting Letter

When writing a prospecting letter for a career change, the cover letter should focus on the reasons for the change and the specific skills and attributes you possess. Here is a sample prospecting letter:

Your Name

Your Address

Your City, State, and Zip Code

Your Phone Number

Your Email

Company Name

Address

City, State, Zip Code

Dear Mr./Ms..........

Subject: Seeking Employment

This letter is to express my interest in discussing the Senior Customer Service Manager position in your organisation. I have learned about your organisation through your website and believe it best suits my career aspirations and where I can contribute. Your organisation profile is appealing, and I believe that my experience and education will make me a competitive candidate for this position.

The key strengths that I possess for success in this position include, but are not limited to, the following:

- Provide exceptional contributions to customer service for all customers.

- Strive for continued excellence.
- Strong communication skills.
- I am a self-starter.
- Eager to learn new things.

You will find me to be well-spoken, energetic, confident, and personable—the type of person on whom your customers will rely. I also have a wide breadth of experience of the type that gives you the versatility to place me in a number of contexts with confidence that the level of excellence you expect will be met. Please see my resume for additional information on my experience.

I hope that you'll find my experience and interests intriguing enough to warrant a face-to-face meeting, as I am confident that I could provide value to you and your customers as a member of your team.

I can be reached anytime via my cell phone, 666-6666666. Thank you for your time and consideration. I look forward to speaking with you about a possible employment opportunity.

Sincerely,

First name, last name

Networking Letter

Your Name

Your Address

Your City, State, Zip Code

Your Phone Number

Your Email

Date

Name

Title

Organization

Address

City, State, Zip Code

Dear Mr. or Mrs. Last Name:

I am writing to solicit your services in finding a suitable vacancy for the position of box office manager in the theatre business.

I am a graduate of the arts with five years of experience in the theatre business. In my present position as Box Office Assistant for the Light Opera Company, I am responsible for customer service, ticketing patrons, and generating and maintaining box office reports. In addition, I maintained records and accounting reports for all box office transactions.

I am a team player who is detailed and has exceptional customer skills. I have good oral and written communication skills.

I am sure that any theatre will find my experience and skills to their advantage and will find me a committed contributor.

I thank you for your assistance in finding a suitable job and look forward to hearing from you soon.

Yours sincerely,

Signature

Another example of a networking letter is:

Contact Name

Title

Company

Address

City, State, Zip

Dear Mr. Contact,

I was referred to you by Diane Khan from XYZ Company in Mumbai. She recommended you as an excellent source of information on the theatre industry.

My goal is to secure a position as box office manager. I would appreciate hearing your advice on career opportunities in the theatre industry, on conducting an effective job search, and on how best to uncover job leads.

Thanks so much, in advance, for any insight and advice you would be willing to share.

Yours sincerely,

Signature

Cover Letter Final Checklist

Before you send your cover letter, review this checklist to make sure that you have covered all the basics and are sending a perfect cover letter to your prospective employer.

- The contact name and company name are correct.
- The letter is addressed to an individual, if possible.
- The letter mentions the position you are applying for and where it was listed.
- Your personal information (as mentioned above) is all included and correct.
- The cover letter is <u>targeted</u> at the position you are applying for.
- The letter is focused, concise (one page only), clear, and well organised.
- If you have a gap in your employment history, you have explained it in your cover letter.
- The font is 10 or 12 points and easy to read (Times New Roman, Verdana, Tahoe, or Arial, for example).
- There are no spelling, grammatical, or typographical errors.
- You have read the cover letter out loud to make sure there are no missing words.
- The cover letter is printed on good-quality bond paper that matches your resume.

- You have kept a copy for your records.
- A letter is signed if you are mailing it.

Note: If you are not fluent in writing in English, get someone who is to do it for you. Make sure you know whatever is written to defend it at the interview. There are professional resume writers.

Four

Preparing for an Interview

PREPARATION TIPS

The hour that you spend preparing for your job interview could be one of the most important activities in your life. It contributes to your career progression, enhances your earning power, and adds to your status in society and the general quality of your life. With such high stakes, it is obvious that you prepare for it thoroughly. You need to have some winning strategies in place so that when you're sitting in that interview room, you put every minute to good use. You need to be as prepared as you can for any number of questions that come your way, and you need to have the right answers at your fingertips so that you exude self-confidence and credibility. Before an interview, ask yourself the question, "Am I prepared?"

Your main goal is to stand out from the rest of the people who are applying for the same position. To do so, follow the tips given below:

Learn about the Organisation

Research and gather background information on the company, its products or services, and its senior management by name before applying. You will need to be prepared to answer the question, "What do you know about our company"? Or "Why do you want to work here?" Knowing as much as possible about the company's past performance and future plans can make your interview more interactive and could be just the leg up you need in a competitive job market. I have rejected many because of their lack of knowledge about the company. They were just blind applicants.

Interest in an organisation can only be exhibited by the amount of knowledge you have about the organisation and the job. From the interviewer's point of view, a good applicant is one who has done some homework prior to coming for the interview. The desirable information that one must possess is:

1. A brief history of the organisation.
2. The organisation's main businesses
3. Nature of the products and services offered by the company
4. Location of its factories, offices, and branches.
5. Any newsworthy issues concerning the organisation.
6. The nature of the job applied for
7. Names of the chairperson and some senior executives
8. What is the current state of the organisation or industry?
9. What are the key problems and issues currently being faced by the organisation?
10. What are the key barriers or roadblocks that stand in the way of solving these problems?
11. What knowledge, skills, and capabilities are needed to remove these barriers?
12. What are the organisation's strategic goals?

13. What new knowledge, skills, and capabilities will be needed to realise these goals?
14. What are the company's expansion plans?
15. What are the growth prospects for the job?
16. Whether they provide training to upgrade skills
17. What is the organisation's culture like?
18. The nature of the job you are applying for and its responsibilities (Job Description)
19. How do you qualify for that position?
20. What are the unique qualities and skills you can bring to the organisation?

Note: Those who are applying to lower positions like technicians, receptionists, security guards, cooks, or other skilled jobs must know at least the products and services of the organisation. The focus will be on their skills.

1. **"Where do I get this information from?"**

   Well, there are many sources from which information can be procured.

   1. The web. Most companies have their own website, giving company background, products and services, locations of their offices and factories, special articles concerning them, etc. Just log on and learn.
   2. Company balance sheets that may be obtained from the company head office (sometimes at a price): Public limited companies publish their balance sheets for their shareholders. It may be difficult to get financial information from private limited companies.
   3. Read the speech of the chairperson at the company's last general body meeting in the case of public limited companies.
   4. Brochures and pamphlets are available from any sales office.

5. Talking to employees of the company through a network of friends.
6. Talking to ex-employees who will give the 'other side' of employment with the company.
7. Visit the showrooms and offices and speak to the receptionist, who may guide you to the right person.
8. See if the company is listed on the stock exchange through the newspaper or financial papers, and learn how much their shares are being quoted at.
9. See back papers for articles on the company about any recent developments.

2. **A Refresher on Your Chosen Subject**

It is natural that the interviewers will quiz you on your chosen field of specialisation. Therefore, if you have studied economics, electrical engineering, human resources, sales and marketing, or whatever, you must go back to the principle textbooks and refresh on the definitions, formulas, concepts, etc. The interviewer assesses your intelligence on the subject and your ability to retain knowledge. Focus on the basics. You must be strong in them.

3. **A Refresher on your Experience**

As the positions that you apply for get higher, it is the experience that counts. Be clear about your job description and the duties and responsibilities that you hold. An important part of preparation for your job is understanding what the new job expects. Information about the new job position can be obtained from:

a. Profile of the job as advertised
b. Talking to job holders in the company through your network of friends
c. Talking to ex-job holders (who may give the negative aspects of the job as well).

You can adapt your answers to the kind of experience they are looking for so as to get an edge over other candidates. Concentrate on your achievements rather than your activities. So if you were able to achieve a 20% increase in sales over the last year, it sounds better than you doing a sales job.

5. **Identify what you have to offer.**

   Your education, training, and experience—what you have done, know how to do, and can do—list down all the skills, abilities, and talents you possess that will make you an excellent employee.

5. **Consider your potential as an employee:**

   * Why do you feel you can do the job?
   * What makes you qualified for the job?
   * What do you have to offer the company or organisation?
   * Why do you want to work for the employer in question?

6. **Practice the frequently asked questions.**

   I have empowered you with frequently asked questions (FAQs) with suggestions of possible answers in Chapter 9. Go through them conscientiously, and it will give you the confidence to face any interview.

7. **Name of the Interviewer/s.**

   Nothing is more precious to a person than his or her name. As part of the preparation process, it would be an added advantage to know the names of those on the selection panel and to address them by their names during the interview. This works like a charm. A rapport is built easily. The interviewer feels recognised and important. The names can be obtained before the interview by asking the person/secretary coordinating the interview. Also, get their designations to give the necessary attention and respect during the interview. It would be an added advantage to recognise them. Therefore, Mr. Mann is the one with the blue suit, while Mr. Paul is the one with the large moustache. The task becomes simpler if there is only one interviewer. Care must be taken to get the name pronunciations correct; otherwise, the effort could become counterproductive.

8. **Keep your documents ready.**

   Documents like the school leaving certificate, college degree, or reference letters are precious to you and are the passport to your future career. I am appalled by the way some candidates keep them. They are kept loosely in plastic bags; they are torn or stained; or they are plain missing. An interviewer evaluates your sense of organisation and meticulousness by the way you maintain and present your documents. Since important documents cannot be punched or stapled, it is best to keep them in files with plastic sleeves. The documents can be tucked into these sleeves. They not only display well but are also saved from disfiguration, water, and stains. The documents must be filed in the sequential order of your education and experience. It helps in easy identification. Make sure that you have another original hard copy of your resume. The interviewer will want an original copy. Also, make sure that all the claims you have made in your resume are well supported by documents. So if you have claimed to have got the "Best Employee of the Year" award for your achievements, then that recognition certificate must be at hand to authenticate your claim. Here is a checklist of documents:

   - School leaving certificate
   - College degree
   - Transcripts
   - Certificates of participation in extra-curricular activities
   - Citations for special accomplishments
   - Work reference letters
   - Character reference letters
   - Certificates of Special courses attended
   - Certificates of recognition

- A fresh copy of your resume
- Copies of all documents

Other unusual documents/artefacts that may be useful are:

- Photographs of recognition ceremonies
- Driving licence
- Project reports
- Medals

9. **Practice Makes Perfect**

   Practice makes perfect (or at least leads to improvement). Practice with a friend or family member. Record or videotape your responses so you can replay the interview and see how well you did. Prepare answers to commonly asked interview questions (found in Chapter 9 of this book). Doing so will help you analyse your background and qualifications for the position. Look into a mirror when rehearsing to show the person the interviewer is seeing. Are you cheerful and confident? Are you well-groomed and smart?

10. **Make a trip to the site of the interview in advance.**

    It is prudent to find the location of the place of the interview in advance. It saves time on the day of the interview. The interviewer is not impressed with a plea, "Sorry I am late, I had difficulty finding the place!" An interviewer hates impunctuality. It is unprofessional, and insulting, and does not value the time of the interviewer. You may wish your candidature goodbye. In my experience at interviews, I had rejected candidates who came late. If I had a series of candidates to interview that day, I would call a late candidate at the end of my interviews. I kept him waiting.

11. **Review your resume.**

    Employers will use your resume as a source of questions during the interview. Review your resume thoroughly prior to the interview and be able to develop answers to questions that relate to your employment and educational experience listed on your resume. Be prepared to discuss gaps in employment. If called upon, you must be able to demonstrate the skills you stated on your resume. Focus on those skills and experience that are relevant to the future job.

PRE-INTERVIEW CHECKLIST:

Check the following before you leave home for your interview:

- Have you researched the organisation you are interviewing with?
- Do you know the interviewer's name? If not, get it from the receptionist before the interview.
- Have you formulated answers for the usual interview questions?
- Do you have all the necessary information for the interview? This includes items such as resume names and addresses of references, pens, and notepads.
- Did you practice the interview with someone? You will benefit from suggestions for improvement.
- Do not forget to research the location of the address BEFORE the interview. What is the company address? How long should you plan for travel time? Drive by the company to be sure that you know how to get there and how long it will take. Also, remember to give yourself an extra 10-15 minutes in case they ask you to complete their job application form.
- Did you consider how the position relates to your talents and goals, such as the specialty area and opportunities for advancement?
- Did you schedule the interview at a time that will not conflict with your working hours? Most interviewers will understand you not wanting to take time off work at your current position to interview for other jobs.
- Did you find out the telephone number of the interviewer in case an emergency arises?
- Are you prepared with answers to why you want to work at that particular organisation, and how you would be the best

candidate for this position? Understanding the company, its mission, and its environment will help you with these questions.

- Did you dress appropriately for the interview? (See the tips in the next chapter).

The night before the interview:

- Check the weather forecast! Will you need an umbrella? Should you wear a coat?
- Decide what you will be taking in your handbag/briefcase and set it aside. Be sure to include a pen and paper, as well as an extra pair of hosiery (for ladies).
- Plan how you will wear your hair and make-up. (You shouldn't try anything new in the morning.) Make-up should be appropriate for daytime, not Saturday night. No glimmer or shimmer, and keep eye makeup to a minimum or wear none at all.
- Check your nails! They should be conservative in length and colour; no chipped polish.
- Do as much of your morning preparation for both yourself and your family as you can.
- Do something to relax: take a warm bath, exercise, etc.
- Have a light dinner (no alcohol) and get to bed early.

Five

The Interview

INTERVIEW ETHICS

Before we proceed to the day of the interview, there are a few ethical considerations to keep in mind.

Go for an interview only when you are sincerely interested in joining the employer.

Provide accurate information on your qualifications and interests. Never falsify data.

Acknowledge the invitation for an on-site or online interview promptly.

Notify employers well in advance (preferably 24 hours) if you must postpone or cancel an interview.

THE INTERVIEW DAY

Having prepared for an interview, the day arrives, and you may have a sense of exhilaration with butterflies in your stomach. The time has come for you to perform. The amount you have prepared will allay your fears correspondingly. But there is always the uncertainty of the unexpected question at the interview. Believe me; the interviewer is also anxious to perform. Her job is on the line. S/he is under pressure to make the right choice and get the person on board as soon as possible. S/he is also challenged to make the job and the organisation attractive to you, especially if you are the right candidate who may have several other job offers. We have already seen that the interview is one of mutuality. As a backdrop, treat the interview as a meeting and not a moment of judgement. Both you and the organisation must match expectations.

Before the interview

- Avoid too much coffee or sugar at breakfast.
- Brush your teeth and put on deodorant!
- Ensure you know the directions to the interview site, the name of the person you are meeting, your hard copy resume, and other relevant items with you.
- Give yourself plenty of time to get there, get comfortable, and find the restroom.
- If you feel nervous, try breathing into the count of ten and then exhale to the count of ten. Try to increase the count.
- Observe your surroundings to get a feel for the workplace.
- Turn off your mobile phone.

Your Dress

What you wear is your signature. Interviewers make first impressions based on how well-groomed you are. Remember that in any career, your image is a powerful communicator. The nonverbal messages your image sends can work in your favour or against you. Your clothing is a primary component of your image and it has its own coded language. Your apparel can signal that you are a leader with winning potential, or it can suggest otherwise. If your clothing is conveying the wrong message, you may need to put in extra effort to command respect and inspire trust.

The key is to project a highly professional image with well-coordinated and impeccably maintained business attire. Immaculate grooming, from your head to your feet, is also essential. It is part and parcel of any position.

People do notice the details of your image and draw assumptions about you. This is particularly true for roles that involve customer contact. I once interviewed a female Public Relations Executive who was stunningly attractive! She could have been a model. I asked her why she was seeking such a high salary, and she explained that the cost of maintaining her image for the position was quite substantial these days. She detailed her expenses on hair care, beauty treatments, special diets, clothing costs, and gym fees. It was a significant investment, but she believed that the organisation placed a premium on how she presented herself in public. I understood her perspective and offered her the job. How you appear can indeed be translated into currency.

Anyone can be perceived as attractive. Yes, anyone. If you pay attention to the finer details of your image, you can project an attractive and professional image, whether you are dressed up or down.

Communication statistics reveal that within only five to thirty seconds, three things are determined about you, whether accurate or false, based on your dress:

1. Your Socioeconomic Status
2. Your Educational Level
3. Your Desirability

Ultimately, we tend to associate well-dressed individuals with intelligence and achievement, and most people prefer to be associated with winners. Therefore, well-dressed and well-groomed individuals are often given more opportunities to prove themselves, increasing their chances of success.

Dressing to impress employers should be a crucial part of your interview strategy. While we may believe that no one should be judged by their attire, the reality is that employers are looking for reasons to eliminate candidates from their selection process. They are not only concerned about your resume and interview performance but also pay attention to the image you project, often forming an impression of your appearance within the first five minutes of meeting you.

They are looking to see if the candidate respects them enough to conform to their perceived expectations. Whether we like it or not, how you dress is taken into consideration in hiring decisions. You want to have a competitive edge, especially when making initial impressions.

Regardless of the job position, it is necessary for men to wear a tailored suit with a tie. These days, it is acceptable to not wear a tie. Those who borrow oversized coats or wear ill-fitting ones can be easily noticed. Most offices are air-conditioned, so a jacket and tie are not out of place. For those starting their career who may not possess a suit, a combination jacket like a blazer is the next best choice. Although combination jackets are more informal than suits, they may still be considered business casual these days. While business casual attire is still acceptable, dressing in a suit for a job interview has never really gone out of style.

Appropriate attire complements your image, and it's important to understand the dress code norms within the industry you are seeking employment. Ties should be coordinated with the suit. If you don't have a suit or combination suit, wearing a tie, at the very least, can add a touch of formality. Your shirt should be crisp and clean, preferably white. For women, wearing Western suits is desirable; however, not everyone can pull them off, so wearing the national dress is perfectly acceptable. It's important to **dress for the position** you are applying for, as the interviewer should be able to visualise you in that role. While formal attire is crucial for front-line or management roles, positions in the back-house, such as storekeepers, factory supervisors, or procurement, can afford to be less formal. It's advisable to avoid wearing overly revealing or provocative clothing. Both male and female candidates should steer clear of jeans and sneakers. Dressing well for the occasion is a sign of respect towards the interviewer. In the service industry, proper grooming is highly valued, as people are an integral part of the product offering. Therefore, grooming is essential. Here are some common tips for grooming:

Tips for a male candidate:

Suit: Opt for a dark, conservative suit in solid, pinstripe, or a subtle plaid pattern.

For an informal business casual environment, consider the following attire:

1. Blazer: Wear a coordinated sport coat or blazer with khakis, chinos, or gabardine trousers.
2. Choose long-sleeved dress shirts in pastel colours such as white, cream, or light blue. Avoid shirts with designs whenever possible. Pin-striped shirts are acceptable as long as the tie is plain.
3. Select medium-width silk ties in solids, stripes, or small patterns. Ensure that the tip of the tie touches the top of the belt and that the upper and lower parts of the tie are aligned perfectly. Coordinate the tie with the trousers.
4. Opt for dressy slip-ons or lace-up shoes in black, burgundy, or dark brown. Wear dark-coloured or neutral over-the-calf socks that coordinate with your trousers. Avoid white sports socks and athletic shoes, even in a casual business environment.
5. Use leather belts in black, burgundy, or dark brown to match your trousers or shoes.
6. Avoid flashy cufflinks, earrings, or neck chains. Choose a trim-styled watch with a leather or good-quality metal strap. Wedding bands and conservative rings are appropriate but limit one per hand.
7. Cover tattoos, maintain a well-groomed haircut, and ensure that your clothes are well-fitting, spotless, and well-ironed.
8. Keep your nails well-manicured and your hands clean.
9. Guard against body odours or the use of cheap perfumes. Consider using effective antiperspirants.
10. Keep your shoes polished and opt for a conservative style. Remember that shoes can convey your personality.

11. If you have facial hair, ensure that it's well-trimmed, especially in a business setting where a close shave is preferable.
12. Maintain good oral hygiene to avoid bad breath. Consider using mint lozenges before the interview.
13. Studies suggest that a metal watch strap can convey strength and power in a business image.
14. Do not chew gum, eat candy, or smoke during the interview.

TIPS FOR A FEMALE CANDIDATE:

1. Preferably wear business suits. If suits don't suit you, consider wearing the national dress (note that the national dress may not be suitable for international assignments). Dresses must be conservative, avoiding bold colours, dramatic prints, low-cut necklines, exposed bra straps, and midriffs. 
2. Skirts should not be above knee length, and dark pants are permissible.
3. Blouses should be in plain colours or feature small, subtle geometric patterns and florals. Avoid sheer fabrics, oversized prints, frills, ruffles, straps, or plunging necklines. Ensure that blouses are well-tailored and consider avoiding sleeveless blouses.
4. Avoid seductive clothing at all costs.
5. Opt for medium to low-heeled pumps for shoes, avoiding open-toe or slingback styles. Shoe colours should be black, navy, taupe, or dark brown leather, matching or being darker than the hemline.
6. Choose belts in neutral colours, no more than an inch wide. Limit your jewellery to small pieces in gold or silver; pearls are also appropriate. Avoid dangling earrings and wear only one pair per ear. Wear your wedding band or one high-quality ring per hand. Avoid trying to impress with excessive jewellery.

7. Select a plain round-face or tank-styled watch with a leather or clasp-style metal band.
8. Maintain your natural hair colour or ensure it appears that way. For longer hair, pull it up or back and away from your face. Ensure your hair is clean, dry, and styled. When in doubt, tying up your hair in a bun looks formal.
9. Keep makeup light and avoid strong perfume. Use deodorant.
10. Cover tattoos.
11. Choose good-quality garments.
12. Ensure that your clothes are clean and well-pressed.
13. Keep fingers and toes manicured and avoid elaborate nail polish designs.
14. Prefer flat shoes over high heels. They should be closed-toed and polished.
15. Avoid going barefoot; wear pants or stockings.
16. Stockings should be clean and preferably beige, tan, or natural colours. They must be free from runs.
17. Light makeup projects a professional work image.
18. Handbags should be conservative in colour, avoiding reds. They should coordinate with your outfit and be small or medium in size.
19. A fresh, light cologne is preferable to a strong one.
20. Opt for long-sleeved blouses; sleeveless is considered too casual.
21. Avoid chewing gum, eating candy, or smoking during the interview.
22. Remove bodily piercings such as nose rings, eyebrow rings, etc., unless they are culturally accepted in the workplace.

Dressing pays off. Take control and go that extra mile in shaping your image. The job market for seekers today is more competitive than ever before, and securing a job may require additional effort.

However, how you should present yourself varies depending on your industry and the specific job you're interviewing for. Here are some industry-specific expectations for eight career areas:

Technology

"If you're applying for a technical position, you won't need a suit," says Carole Martin, a former Monster contributor and author of Boost Your Interview IQ. "A collared shirt and khakis or slacks would work. The same goes for women - a sweater or blouse with slacks or a skirt."

But upgrade your attire if you're interviewing for a higher-level job. "You should dress in the best clothes you have," says David Perry, managing director of Perry-Martel International, a high-tech recruiting firm based in Ottawa, Canada, and author of Career Guide for the High-Tech Professional. "No exceptions."

Finance

"Nothing is more precise and exact than managing money," says Pamela Holland, chief operating officer for Brody Communications in Jenkintown, Pennsylvania, and coauthor of Help! Was That a Career Limiting Move? "You cannot afford to have a hair out of place. Full business professional attire is required and expected."

Government

At a government interview, "Don't be flashy," advises Holland. "This is a time to show that you're responsible, trustworthy, and honest."

But a bit of colour is acceptable, whether you're a man or a woman, says Kathryn Troutman, Monster Federal Career Coach and author of Ten Steps to a Federal Job. "Be conservative with jewellery, makeup, and hairstyles," advises Troutman. "Maintain an overall conservative appearance." However, "the days of all-white shirts for men in government need to end," she adds.

Human Resources

When attending an HR interview, "you must look professional and authoritative," states Martin. "You'll need to convey the look that you can handle any crisis and be dependable."

Sales

Typically, a suit is the uniform for a sales interview. After all, as Martin stresses, "Who would want to buy from a guy in a T-shirt and jeans?"

However, you might be able to go with bolder designs and colours, says Holland. "The product or service you're representing will determine how classic versus trendy/fashionable you should be," she explains.

Automotive

"Here's an exception where a potential employer will understand if you have a little dirt or grease under your nails," notes Holland. "You still want to look as neat as possible, but a suit is probably not necessary."

That is unless you're interviewing at a high-end dealership, says Heidi Nelson, a personnel counsellor for Car People Oregon, a Portland, Oregon, automotive staffing service for new-car dealerships. In that case, Nelson says, "I would dress up a bit more."

Hospitality

Image is particularly critical in the hospitality industry. A suit is a must for most guest contact positions. Remember that they will provide you with a uniform and want to see how well you present yourself. However, you always need to make a great initial impression. In hospitality, you are the product, as people provide the service. Your grooming is part of the total sales package.

Trades

John Coffey worked as a factory production manager for years before becoming a career coach. His take on appropriate attire for an interview in the trades: Business casual.

"For men, this might be a nice pair of Dockers and a buttoned shirt, along with well-kept and polished shoes," says Coffey, career success officer for Winning Careers in Woodbury, Minnesota. "The same goes for women - nice slacks and a professional business top. I think a suit or sports jacket for this type of work is overkill."

Of course, what is considered excess in one industry might be viewed as underdressed in another. So, don't be afraid to ask because, no matter what, "Your packaging counts," says Holland.

In my experience, I have observed grooming issues that worked against candidates, such as:

- Dishevelled hair
- Long hair growing from the nose
- Unstyled hair for women
- Unclean spectacles
- Dirt at the corners of the eyes
- Ill-fitting clothes
- Wearing a tie with a missing collar button
- Dirty and dog-eared collars
- Dirt lining the collar of the shirt
- Unpressed clothes
- Missing buttons on the shirt
- Dirty bra straps for women
- Shirt cuffs without buttons
- Dirty hands
- Dirty nails
- Chipped nail polish for women
- Casual shoes
- Body odour

These flaws create negative impressions and distract the interviewer. They convey a personality that is imperfect, lacks personal standards, has poor hygiene, and appears too casual for such an important meeting.

Being on time

Interviewers set aside time from their busy schedules to meet with you. Interviews are time-consuming and require careful planning. When you keep an interviewer waiting, it can be infuriating. It is insulting and may give the impression of disinterest, even if it's not the case. Failing to arrive on time can significantly harm your chances of securing the job.

The first step in the right direction is to arrive at the interview venue at least ten minutes early. Remember that you have already visited the site as part of your preparations, so you should be familiar with the location. Use this time to visit the restroom to freshen up and look your best for the interview. By doing so, you win the first round!

Self-Motivation

While waiting for the interview, motivate yourself. Remind yourself that you are a remarkable individual and believe in your abilities because if you don't, no one else will. Create your own path in life and then go out and live it.

MY FRIEND, YOU ARE EXTRAORDINARY!! The odds are greater than 50 million to 1 against there ever being anyone with the unique combination of talents, skills, and abilities that you possess. The remarkable achievements you are capable of, no one knows, not even yourself.

Exploit your strengths and starve your weaknesses. "WE ARE WHAT WE THINK WE ARE!" You must make up your mind to look at yourself honestly and make future decisions based on your uniqueness.

To have a positive day, keep the following in mind:

- Every problem has a solution.
- Failures always lead to learning something you can use later.
- Many times you must take a step back before you take two steps forward.

* After a crisis, there is always an opportunity.
* You control your thoughts and feelings.
* You make the choices that determine your fate.

Obstacles don't have to stop you. If you run into a wall, don't turn around and give up. Figure out how to climb it, go through it, or work around it.

Waiting for Your Turn

Very often, you may be required by the interviewing organisation to wait with other candidates in an adjoining room before your turn. This often occurs at entry-level or junior positions. Senior positions are handled more discreetly and with greater confidentiality. During this waiting period, you can use your time productively to enhance your chances in the interview.

1. Introduce yourself to other candidates and initiate conversation. This allows you to assess your competition, their attitudes, and confidence levels. You may come across some topics or issues that you should have prepared for. Keep in mind that some organisations may have psychologists in the room to study candidate behaviour. You should aim to be seen as a leader, extroverted, and confident.
2. Often, the secretary or the person coordinating the interview is present in the room. Try to engage in a conversation with them to ascertain the names of the interviewers and how to identify them. You can also inquire about information regarding the organisation, the job, and possibly when the interview results will be known. It's possible that the organisation's representative in the room will provide feedback to the interviewers about your confidence and enthusiasm.
3. Ask for literature about the organisation that you can quickly review for additional information. Remember that you have already done some preliminary research beforehand, which reflects your keenness and initiative toward the organisation's representatives in the room.

4. Make sure you know the correct name and pronunciation of the interviewer. Listen carefully when the interviewer states their name and repeat it when you greet them. Before you leave, request a business card from each person you meet. This provides you with the necessary information to send thank-you letters.

THE INTERVIEW

You are called into the interview room. The moment of truth has arrived. This is what you have been preparing for. Most interviews can be divided into four major sections: the introduction, the candidate sell, the employer sell, and the closing.

During the "introduction," the employer will use the first few minutes of the interview to create a comfortable, friendly environment so that a meaningful conversation can follow. A mutual topic of discussion, such as the weather, sports, or a major news story, will normally be pursued.

The "candidate sell" is the time spent answering questions about your goals and qualifications and demonstrating your communication skills.

The "employer sell" will cover organisational structure, products or services, geographical location(s), specifics on the position under consideration, salary (usually not discussed during an initial interview), benefits, etc.

During the "closing," both parties should indicate their level of interest in the other and understand what the next steps to be taken will be.

Here is a step-by-step sequence to follow:

INTRODUCTION

1. Thank the representative who called you in.
2. Adjust your dress before entering. Keep your documents in your left hand to enable you to open the interview room door and shake hands.
3. Knock the door lightly before opening it. Often the representative will open the door for you.

4. Wear a smile. Nothing is more captivating and refreshing to an interviewer than someone who smiles. It sets a cordial tone for the interview.

5. Seek permission to enter by saying, "May I enter, sir/Madam (preferably use their name)?"

6. Shut the door behind you while facing the interviewer. (This will need practice).

7. Enter the room walking upright. Some organisations keep a distance between the door and the interview table. Don't be intimidated. They want to see your dress and gait while walking.

8. At the table, the interviewer may offer a handshake. Give a firm handshake. A limp handshake tells you you are characterless and without a spine. A very strong handshake may give the impression that you are very aggressive or insecure but it creates an impression. A sweaty hand shows you are nervous. A firm handshake shows your confidence. Practice your handshake before coming for the interview with your relatives or friends. Let them tell you how your handshake is. In some communities, women interviewers do not offer a handshake. Respect that. You can bow gently while wishing them.

9. Sit only after being given permission to do so. Choosing to sit without permission shows insolence. Should the interviewer forget this formality, ask politely, "May I sit please?"

10. Sit upright in the chair. Place your document file before you on the table and your hands clasped on your lap. Remember that unlocked hands can go astray when talking. The gestures can be distracting and can even give away your feelings. I have noticed trembling hands. Others tend to play with their ties, hair, or clothes. Keep your knees together.

11. The first task of an interviewer is to break the ice. Good interviewers will start with light talk to put you at ease. Use that cue to relax. Some will choose your hobby as a starting point for discussion. They do this in the belief that you would be most comfortable discussing hobbies. Remember that you have listed the hobby(s) that you are

most accomplished in. Impress the interviewer with your knowledge on the subject. Speak with enthusiasm. It is infectious and carries to the interviewer.

The enthusiasm comes with the energetic (not excitable) way you present your thoughts. You should maintain a cheerful disposition throughout the interview. This does not mean that you should be casual or frivolous. It simply means that a pleasant countenance holds the interviewer's attention. It is a good way to make an impression. Some interviewers may not know how to start the interview. You may notice a long pause as they scan your resume, searching for a starting point. Well, you could help the interviewer by saying, "May I give you a synopsis of my resume?" or "Shall I tell you about my academic achievements?" Some candidates are very good at breaking the ice. They pick up a clue from the office like my business degree hung on the wall or a gold artefact on the desk. Each personal office of an interviewer has many clues, and a good candidate will pick up on these and talk about them, such as "I see you are a golfer. Which golf club do you play at?" or "That's an impressive certificate you have on the wall!" The conversation is initiated on that topic that sets the wheels of the interview process.

Candidate Sell

12. ***Be brief.*** Answer questions posed to you concisely and to the point. I have listed 101 frequently asked questions in Chapter 9. Go through them in your preparations.

13. ***Don't bluff.*** If you do not know the answer to a question, it is better to acknowledge that you don't know the answer than bluffing your way through it. In my experience, the interviewer will immediately grill a candidate if they suspect the candidate of lying. The interviewer will respect your integrity and honesty. Bluffing should not be necessary if you have prepared well for the interview.

14. ***Lead the interview.*** It may come as a surprise to you that many interviewers are not trained to conduct interviews. They are quite shy and are sometimes lost for questions to ask. You should be quick to sense this. Indications are a long pause between questions or when interviewers are shuffling through the resume. This pause is enough to suggest, "May I tell you about my experience?" or something to that effect. The interviewer will, more often than not, welcome the suggestion. Trained interviewers would have studied your resume in advance and written down specific questions to ask you. Normally, they look for answers not listed in the resume. Untrained interviewers will more often than not ask you questions by repeating what is already listed in the resume. Perhaps you can suggest some issues about yourself that do not find a place in the resume. Such issues could be details of your hobbies or interests, your long-term goals and aspirations, or details of your achievements. You can suggest these to lead the interview rather than being a dumb onlooker. Many candidates believe they are there to answer questions only. What is required is a more proactive approach where you want to tell the interviewer what you want them to know. You can suggest, for example, "May I tell you about the special project that I did in XYZ company where I got recognition?" or "May I tell you how I reduced the costs of operations in my last job?" Showcase your strengths and achievements. The interview discussion then could enter into areas that you are comfortable and confident about.

15. ***Sell yourself.*** There is an element of salesmanship in each interview. Consider yourself as the 'product' with the aim of convincing the interviewer to 'buy' your services.

16. ***Listen carefully.*** It is a skill that can work to your benefit. Firstly, you will understand the question being asked. Secondly, it opens the opportunity for a two-way conversation. Thirdly, it shows your composure and gives you the time to mentally prepare your answers using your mental capacity, which works four times faster than what is spoken.

17. ***Keep the interviewer's attention*** and interest in you. Some interviewers may have interviewed all day and reached a level of fatigue. They

may have grown tired of asking the same questions. A tired interviewer can be challenging because they might have switched off and not be giving you the opportunity to showcase yourself. If you notice this, there are many ways to rouse the interviewer's interest: a) You can vary the tone of your voice. A monotonous drone can lull the interviewer into sleep! b) Vary the speed of your speech. Speak faster to show excitement, interspersed with slow diction to emphasise a point. c) Bring the interviewer's attention to your documents. d) Talk about the interviewer's own interests, as mentioned earlier; etc. In other words, any change in behaviour may create something new.

18. ***Be Enthusiastic.*** The interviewer normally pays more attention if you display enthusiasm in whatever you say. This enthusiasm comes across in the energetic way you put forward your ideas. You should maintain a cheerful disposition throughout the interview. A pleasant countenance holds the interviewer's interest.

19. ***Use humour.*** A person good at it must use it at the interview. It does not mean telling jokes but using wit. This is especially helpful in awkward situations. Two examples stand out in my experience: A candidate tripped while entering the interview hall. He said, "I've sure stumbled into good company!" A female candidate dropped her testimonials when approaching me. She said, "There you are, I have spilled the beans about myself already." If you are not skilled at humour, do not attempt it. Poorly told jokes are worse than not telling them at all.

20. ***Show loyalty*** to your previous organisations, even if you left them in unsavoury circumstances. A common question asked by interviewers is, "Why did you leave your previous organisation?" Never speak negatively about your past employer. Instead, provide reasons such as your own career aspirations, long commuting distances, or seeking new challenges. Demonstrating loyalty to your previous employers can reassure the prospective employer about your professionalism and discretion, essential qualities when handling confidential information and processes.

21. **Avoid slang and jargon.** Slang consists of popular words not found in the English dictionary, often coined for casual conversation. While slang may be part of daily communication, it is inappropriate in a formal interview setting. Your communication should maintain a high level of formality to convey professionalism. Jargon, on the other hand, comprises technical terms used in specific professions. Using jargon can be problematic in interviews, especially if the interviewer is not familiar with the terms being used. IT professionals, for example, may inadvertently use technical jargon that the interviewer does not understand. It's essential to gauge the interviewer's familiarity with industry-specific terms and provide explanations as needed to ensure clear communication.

22. ***Avoid smoking, chewing gum, or consuming candy*** during interviews. Many workplaces have designated "no smoking" areas, and some individuals may have allergies or religious objections to smoking. Additionally, some organisations prefer to hire non-smokers because of concerns that smokers may take breaks for smoking. While some interviewers may offer cigarettes as a courtesy, it is advisable to decline politely. Maintaining formality during the interview process is generally preferred.

23. ***Show manners***; they are very important. They reflect your upbringing and culture. Words that show manners include: "Yes, please!" "I beg your pardon," "Thank you," "I wish to state," etc. Actions also convey manners, such as knocking on the door before entering, seeking permission to enter, sitting only when invited, shaking hands, and greeting the interviewer.

24. ***Maintain poise during the interview.*** Poise is how you carry your body while walking or sitting; it should be upright. Your body conveys non-verbal messages, popularly referred to as body language. For example, if you cross your arms and clutch yourself, it shows insecurity and closedness. If you sit with your body facing away from the interviewer, it indicates non-cooperation and suspicion. If you fling your arms over the back of your chair, it signifies overconfidence or a 'couldn't care less' attitude. Crossing your legs suggests you are on guard and defensive, while trembling hands and fingers betray nervousness.

Proper sitting posture has already been explained. Good interviewers position the interview chair at a distance from the table to observe your body language. Some even forgo a table in between and opt for an open seating arrangement, like a sofa.

25. ***Maintain eye contact;*** it is another form of body language. I have singled this out as it is an important aspect of your personality. Eye contact with the interviewer demonstrates self-confidence, honesty, and veracity. The lack of eye contact indicates untruthfulness, fear, and lack of confidence. Maintaining eye contact can be challenging, especially for women in many cultures who are trained not to look into the eyes of men as a sign of humility, respect, and coyness. However, an interviewer may accept these deviations if they have thoroughly studied the candidate. Eye contact is essential for making a positive impression.

26. ***Seek clarifications*** for questions that you do not understand by asking, "Excuse me, sir, could you please repeat the question?" The interviewer may rephrase the question to help you better understand it. Nothing is more frustrating for an interviewer than receiving an unrelated answer because the candidate did not grasp the question initially.

27. ***Be natural.*** Sometimes, candidates adopt an accent that they cannot sustain throughout the interview. Interviewers appreciate authenticity rather than an artificial persona, which they can easily discern. Be yourself while maintaining the formal postures and manners appropriate for the occasion.

28. ***Show your reliability.*** The interview serves as the first test of your dependability, so ensure that you arrive on time (even better, a few minutes early). You are conveying to the employer that you will consistently arrive punctually for work, complete tasks, collaborate effectively with colleagues and can be trusted.

Employer's Sell

29. ***Ask questions.*** We have already learned that an interview is a dialogue of mutuality. Do not consider yourself as a victim, and the interviewer as the almighty. This kind of belief will only stunt the full potential

of the interview. You must not forget that the organisation treats the interview with equal importance as they must fill the job with the right person just as much as you want the job. It is therefore important that both the interviewer and you jointly create conditions in an interview to bring about the mutuality of purpose. Your contribution towards the process is to ask questions to see if the organisation and job suit you. Some questions that can be asked are:

- The organisation's mission and objectives
- The organisation's values (that define the culture)
- Career prospects
- Nature of the job
- Who you will be reporting to
- Working conditions
- Terms of employment
- The next step in the recruitment process
- When you expect to hear from the organisation
- How much notice period you will need to join
- Facilities and benefits that the organisation offers, e.g., transportation, housing, medical, superannuation, meals during office hours, staff canteen, etc.
- What will be my biggest challenge if I get the job?
- What is it in my resume that attracted me to you?
- What things do you expect me to accomplish if you give me this job?
- What level of responsibility can I expect in this position?
- Why is this job available?
- What training programmes do you have for new employees?
- Is there a typical career path for a person in this position?

- How are employees evaluated?
- Tell me about a typical day in this department.

Don't forget to ask questions that involve the management of others if you're seeking a supervisory or management position. Some of these questions include: (1) How much authority will I have to run my own department? (2) How many employees will I be supervising? (3) May I please see the company organisational chart? (4) Will any employees be let go or transferred from my department?

The better prepared you are to ask questions at the end of your interview, the bigger impact you'll leave on your interviewer. Questions demonstrate your interest in the job and show that you have taken the time to prepare for the interview.

30. ***Salary negotiation.*** This is perhaps the most awkward moment for both you and the interviewer. However, this need not be the case. Every interviewer understands that your interest in the job is dependent on your salary expectations. Many organisations may have advertised their salary in the job posting, in which case you would have already seen it when applying. On the other hand, some organisations keep salary details confidential and prefer to discuss them during the interview. It is not impolite to inquire about your remuneration terms. In fact, interviewers expect you to inquire about the salary.

    When you inquire about the salary terms, you can expect the following responses:

    - "We will discuss it at the next stage of the recruitment process," which means they want to keep the salary details confidential until they are certain about recruiting you.
    - "What do you expect?" is an indication that the salary is negotiable, and they want to determine if your expectations align with what they can offer. In such a situation, it's advisable to share your current salary and express your expectation for an increase to justify the move. Typically, a 25-30% increase is considered acceptable. If their offer exceeds your current salary, they are likely to inform you immediately. Otherwise, they may need time to evaluate whether they can meet your expectations.

- "Your CTC (Cost to Company) will be..." Nowadays, companies often provide a lump sum, allowing you to decide how to allocate your salary for tax planning. The organisation may specify the basic salary to align with the company's salary structure, as it also affects leave pay, medical benefits, and superannuation benefits.

While salary is a highly individual matter, it should be considered in its entirety. This includes factors such as the benefits and perks offered in addition to the salary, the prospects for career growth where you may be willing to accept a lower current remuneration for the opportunity for substantial future progress, the company's commitment to training and how they intend to enhance your value over time, the quality of work life encompassing aspects like working hours, weekend breaks, annual holidays, family-related facilities, the prevailing work culture, the level of empowerment granted to perform your role, and the recognition and reward systems in place. Moreover, consider the convenience of working with the organisation while maintaining a balance with your personal life.

Closing the Interview

31. The way you conclude the interview is as vital as the main body of the interview. It is the parting impression that you leave prior to the interview. The following statement should typify a good ending: "I thank you, sir/madam, for providing me this opportunity for an interview. I look forward to hearing from you again." You should then rise and wish the time of the day with a handshake, maintaining eye contact. Remember to address the interviewer by name. Open the door while facing the interviewer and shut the door quietly behind you. Often, the interviewer will lead you to the door as a courtesy. Wish him or her again when exiting.

32. It is prudent to stay a while in the outer office in case the interviewer has an afterthought and wishes to speak to you. It is imperative to wish the secretary or interview coordinator before leaving. Let me tell you that they play a big part in influencing decisions because they see you 'off guard' and can provide another perspective.

If you're working on your education so that you can get one of those jobs, you might want to apply just for the experience. The important thing to remember is that you are realistic about your chances of getting the job. Many employers want to hire people when they are at the beginning of their career so that they can shape them and guide them in the direction that they need. This can work to your advantage if you're just out of university and are looking for an entry-level job. Other employers want to hire people who have the education as well as the experience that they are looking for. This often means fewer training costs for the company. When you go to your job interview, be realistic about the knowledge and the experience that you have. You may not always get the job, but every interview should be a learning experience that prepares you for the next one.

Why do candidates get rejected?

In my experience with interviews over the years and by asking other interviewers, here are some common reasons why candidates get rejected:

Resume:

- Poorly formatted resume
- Untidy resume
- Incomplete resume
- Stated profile unsuitable for the job
- Underqualified/overqualified
- Poor or missing cover letter

Personality:

- Poorly dressed and ill-groomed
- Lack of courtesy and manners
- Lack of confidence
- Aggressive and flashy

* Dishonest
* Lack of tact and diplomacy
* Immaturity
* Lack of sincerity
* Artificial
* Lack of vitality
* No eye contact
* Feeble handshake
* Name-dropper (uses influential names to get selected)
* Uses parental influence
* Lazy
* Low moral standards
* Non-punctual
* Extreme ideas and values
* Not a team player
* Bluffer
* Poor posture and sloppiness
* Casual approach
* Disrespectful
* Clock-watcher (more interested in the number of hours than job completion)
* Restless and fidgety
* Proud and aloof
* Does not fit in with the organisation's culture
* Strong prejudices
* Overbearing and arrogant
* Immaturity

Interview Process:

* Late for the interview
* Does not shut the door
* Sits without permission
* Poor poise
* Unable to comprehend questions
* Disorganised answers
* Superficial answers
* Unconvincing answers to questions
* Does not ask questions
* Criticism of past employers
* Evasive in answering some questions
* No knowledge of the new organisation

Communication:

* Poor communication skills
* Poor listener
* Uses slang and jargon
* Inaudible
* Speaks too loudly
* Lack of humour
* Uses gesticulations to express
* Rude
* Excitable when expressing

Motivation:

- Overemphasis on money rather than growth
- Lack of career goals
- Overambitious
- Unrealistic aspirations

Job Knowledge and Experience:

- Lack of job knowledge
- Lack of experience
- Not committed to the profession
- Lack of past achievements
- More bookish than hands-on
- Has not recently upgraded themselves
- Lack of product knowledge

Personal Circumstances:

- Disturbed family circumstances
- No mobility in transfers due to family commitments
- Inflexible with time
- Residence far away from the office
- Has no personal transport (for outdoor sales jobs)
- Joining time from the previous job is far too long
- Does not possess a passport (for overseas assignments)
- Poor health
- Under or over-aged
- Salary expectations too high
- No career plan

Of course, even great questions will not secure you a job offer if you come in with other problems. Here, in order, are the ten attitude strikeouts that most often condemn job candidates:

- Doesn't ask questions
- Condemnation of past employer
- Inability to accept criticism
- Poor personal appearance
- Indecisiveness, cynicism, laziness
- Overbearing, over-aggressive, "know-it-all" attitude
- Arriving late for the interview
- Failure to maintain eye contact with the interviewer
- Difficulty in expressing oneself clearly
- Overemphasis on money

Six

Techniques that Interviewers Employ

This chapter would be the most useful to you as I am giving you a view from the other side of the table. You will see the techniques interviewers employ to extract information from you. I have often heard candidates proclaiming that they have done well at an interview but were shocked and disappointed when they were not selected. What went wrong? The failure, in all probability, lay in the techniques employed by the interviewer and the trap that the candidate fell into unknowingly. Here is a glimpse from the other side of the table:

1. **While Waiting**

   Interview Technique

   Your assessment could well start while waiting in the foyer before entering the interview room. Be ready. Modern offices may have a CCTV (closed-circuit TV) where a camera is positioned in the foyer, and the interviewer observes you on their monitor. Alternatively, a receptionist/secretary is positioned to coordinate the interview. They may be 'planted' to observe your behaviour while waiting.

   Your Tactic

   Try to strike up a friendly conversation with the receptionist with small talk. Try to find out about the organisation and the name of the interviewer if not known. You could also ask for the company brochure to browse through while waiting. If there are other candidates, make friends with them. It shows your confidence and people orientation. Don't just sit there. If nothing else, review your resume and make notes. Sit upright. The interviewer will observe the following:

- Your congeniality
- Your dress
- Your posture
- Your active disposition
- Your eagerness to know more about the organisation

2. **Entry**

Interviewer Technique

The interviewer maintains a distance between the door and the interview table. It is said that interviewers form an opinion within the first 30 seconds and thereafter try to defend that opinion. It is unfortunate but a reality. Let us hope that the first impression is a positive one. If the impression is bad, then you will have to perform outstandingly to overcome the initial negative impression. The first thirty seconds are largely spent on your entry and greeting. The impact must be outstanding to shape the initial opinion.

Your Tactic

Ensure that you have groomed impeccably, as explained earlier. Apply a touch of deodorant or a light cologne. Smell pleasant. The tap on the door should be firm but not too loud. Seek permission to enter by simply saying, "May I enter, Sir/Madam?" If you have learned the name of the interviewer, then use it while seeking permission to enter. It immediately breaks barriers. Once granted permission, close the door behind you. Interviewers get annoyed when the door is left open. You should not hear, "Please close the door behind you!" While closing the door, do so softly while facing the interviewer. Walk erect to the interview table with a smile. The smile conveys your confidence and eases the tension in the room. The interviewer is likely to smile back at you. Some may not—don't be concerned; they might be trying to put pressure on you.

Greet the interviewer, saying, "Good morning, Mr/Ms ....., nice to meet you." If you do not know the name of the interviewer/s, address them as Sir/Madam. Offer a firm handshake if the interviewer offers it. Wait to be given permission to sit. Sit with your back upright against the back of the chair, with your knees together and your hands clasped on your lap. You may place your document folder on your lap.

At this point, the interviewer has already formed initial impressions of you, including:

* Well-groomed (would be a good representative of our company)
* Polite with manners (can be trusted with our clients)
* Pleasant fragrance (indicating good personal hygiene)
* Firm handshake (a sign of confidence)
* Knowledge of my name (shows effort in preparation)
* Upright posture (displays a person with spine)

3. **Seating**

Interviewer Technique

Sometimes, the interviewer will place a desk or table between the two of you. This arrangement may be intended to establish the interviewer's authority, as they may enjoy asserting their superior position. They might position your chair at a distance from the table to observe your posture and assess the volume of your voice from that distance. Unprepared candidates may feel intimidated. It's essential not to move your chair closer to the desk. All the interviewer wants is respect. Some candidates prefer having the table in between; it can act as psychological 'protection' from the barrage of questions.

Better-trained interviewers may opt for a sofa seating arrangement without a table in between. The goal here is to create a more casual environment, making you feel less intimidated and more relaxed. However, some candidates may feel 'exposed' in such a seating arrangement and, therefore, uncomfortable. It's worth noting that interviewers sometimes pause to see whether you seek permission to sit.

Your Tactic

First, wait for the interviewer to give you permission to sit. Your posture is key here. Sit upright with your back against the chair, keeping your knees together and hands on your lap. Place your documents on the table. Low sofas can be problematic if there's a tendency to slouch. In such a case, sit upright at the edge of the sofa with your documents and hands clasped on your lap. Regardless of the seating, always show respect to the interviewer and demonstrate confidence by smiling. The interviewer will make the following mental notes about you:

- Good posture
- Confidence (not easily intimidated)

4. **Putting at Ease**

Interviewer's Technique

The moment you sit, the interviewer will ask light questions to put you at ease. You may hear questions like, "Did you have difficulty finding this place?" or "I see that you are a cricket enthusiast!" or "The weather has been bad recently, hasn't it?" The intention is to start the conversation and break the ice. This first question could be asked within the first 30 seconds before forming an impression.

Your Tactic

Recognise the question and its purpose. Be concise in your response, but avoid simple "yes" or "no" answers. Your initial comments could set the tone for the interview. Convert such a question to your advantage. For example, in response to the first question, you could say, "No, Mr. ... I made sure to visit the location a few days ago to ensure I wouldn't be late for this interview." This response shows that you took the initiative to locate the site and were punctual—a strong start to the interview. Opening questions about your hobbies and interests provide an opportunity to showcase your knowledge on the subject. Impress them with the depth of your information. The interviewer will value your commitment to your interests and believe that you will continue this trait in your job if hired. For the third question, you could respond with, "I am an all-weather person!" Naturally, these answers should have been rehearsed during your interview preparation. Maintain a cheerful demeanour while answering.

At this Stage, the Interviewer Would Have Assessed the Following:

- Your communication skills
- Your positive thinking
- Your flow of thought and logic
- Your commitment to interests and hobbies
- Your cheerfulness
- Your amiability
- Your interest
- Your thoroughness

5. **Question Techniques**

Interviewer's Techniques

An interviewer employs an array of question techniques to obtain the information they seek. Essentially, there are three question techniques:

1. **Closed Questions:** These are used by interviewers to obtain specific information and can typically be answered with a "yes" or "no" or a single sentence. They are often used to verify facts or clarify details from your resume. Such questions usually start with words like "Do," "Have," "Will," etc. Examples of closed questions include: "Do you have to serve a notice period?" or "Have you obtained a certificate?" or "Will you be leaving town in the next fortnight?" These questions can be answered with a simple "yes" or "no."

2. **Open Questions:** These questions are asked to elicit maximum information from you and to assess your knowledge on a subject. They typically start with words like "What," "Where," "Which," "When," "Why," and "How." Open questions cannot be answered with a simple "yes" or "no." Examples of open questions include: "Why do you wish to leave your current job?" or "What are your current responsibilities?" or "When do you plan to join if selected?" or "How do you plan to commute to the office from your current location?" These questions require detailed responses.

3. **Hypothetical Questions:** Hypothetical questions are used to assess your analytical ability. These questions often start with "If," "Suppose," or "Imagine." Examples of hypothetical questions include: "If you were selected, what would you do on your first day?" or "Suppose you had to assemble a project team, how would you go about it?" or "Imagine that your equipment broke down, what emergency methods would you employ?" These questions are designed to evaluate your analytical skills, logic, and ability to apply your experience to various scenarios.

Your Tactic

Recognise these questions. Open questions require detailed but concise explanations. Avoid being overly verbose. As for hypothetical questions, there may not be specific answers to them. The interviewer is evaluating your logical thought process and how well your experience can be applied to the situations described.

6. Listening

Interviewer's Technique

A skilled interviewer tends to speak less and encourages you to speak more. They are attentive listeners and carefully evaluate every word you utter. When they ask a question, the interviewer utilises their mental capacity, as mentioned earlier, to understand, analyse, and assess your responses.

Your Tactic

Pay attention to the posture and expression of the interviewer while responding. Your success can be gauged by the interviewer's eye contact, nods of the head, smiles, and even leaning forward while listening to you. Lack of interest may be indicated by a break in eye contact, fidgeting with objects on the table, leaning back in boredom, yawning, or interrupting your discourse. It is crucial that the interviewer maintains interest throughout. If you sense a loss of interest, you can recapture it by modulating your voice, changing the direction of your topic, or asking a question such as, "Would you like me to continue?" Enthusiasm is a surefire way to engage your interviewer.

7. **Interview fatigue**

This is a common ailment for most interviewers, especially those who have been having back-to-back interviews throughout the day. They do break the monotony between interviews by taking a walk, sending important e-mails, making phone calls, ordering coffee, or visiting the cloak room. But if the fatigue sets in during the interview, they would prefer to stand and interview you, pace up and down the room, order black coffee, etc. One effective technique employed by interviewers is to ask open-ended questions to get the candidate to talk more, giving them a break from questioning. It is the timing of these questions that distinguishes between probing questions and 'break' questions, which come towards the end of the interview. Fatigue questions can descend from the serious to the lighthearted, such as "Tell me about yourself," "What are your strengths and weaknesses?" or "How was your college life?" Sometimes they break the interviewing process by asking to see your certificates.

Your Tactic

Recognise the interviewer's fatigue. Symptoms would be slumping in the chair, tired gestures, walking up and down the room, drying up in questions, idly thumbing through your resume, or ordering coffee. The interviewer may ask you to join in having coffee.

Refuse the offer because the interviewer wants to be in control of time and does not want to lengthen the interview process with you having to finish the coffee. Interview fatigue does not mean taking things easy. Remember, the interviewer is tired, not you. This is a golden time to suggest questions to the interviewer, such as "Would you like me to tell you about my achievements in my last job?" The interviewer would welcome it, especially if s/he is dried up with questions to ask. Remember, the interviewer is listening, and now is the time to be enthusiastic and give a good account of yourself. Enthusiasm can be energising for both of you. Even when posed with a lighthearted question, as mentioned before, treat it seriously and answer it to the best of your ability. Humour is magic in such situations. Making the interviewer laugh is energising. But use humour only if you are good at it.

8. Evaluating Personal Qualities

Interviewer's techniques

Employers look for more than technical or specific job-related skills when hiring new employees. Employers look for these characteristics during the hiring process through observation and questioning techniques. Knowing these characteristics and being able to identify them in yourself will enhance your success at interviews and increase your chances of getting the job that you desire.

For an interviewer to identify your strengths in these areas, they need to ask behaviour-based or situational questions such as "Tell me about a time when you had a conflict with a co-worker and how you resolved it." This type of question is becoming more and more common in interviews.

Many more employers are asking "behavioural questions" in the job interview. This means that rather than focusing on your resume and your accomplishments, the interview will focus more on questions that are open-ended. This means that there won't be one single right answer to a question but a wide spectrum of answers instead. You'll be given real-life circumstances, and your response to these situations is what your interviewer will be looking at. You can share your experiences.

For instance, you might be asked to describe a certain event, experience, or project. You may have to talk about how you handled a particular situation and what the end result was. The goal behind this type of interview is to rate your performance in everyday situations that may arise while you're on the job. Your experience will count.

Your interviewer will be asking you questions that require detail, understanding, and depth in your response. For example, you might be asked "What were you thinking when that happened" or "Tell me more about how you handled that incident and why"; "Talk about the riskiest decision that you've made"; "Describe a time where you were in danger of missing a deadline"; or "Give an example of a bad decision that you've made and what the end result was". These questions require that you take a moment to think about your answer before you open your mouth.

Manners: Apart from the entry manners explained earlier, they also notice whether you say words like "please," "thank you", "I beg your pardon", "kindly," and "excuse me". Use these words regularly. They are cheap but get you a lot of mileage.

Loyalty: A question such as "Why are you leaving your present organisation?" or "Tell me about your boss" is full of intention. They want to see if you let down your previous organisation or uphold it. Interviewers like a person who fiercely defends his or her previous organisation because it implies that you would do the same with their organisation. Answer by saying, "I wanted a new experience", "I got an offer I couldn't refuse" and "I was looking for a job that was closer to my talents".

Job-hopper: No organisation likes a job-hopper. A job-hopper is one who changes jobs very frequently. If you are a person who has changed jobs frequently, then beware, because any interviewer will fear that you will do the same to them if you join. Unfortunately, in present times, millennials change jobs frequently for better remuneration. This applies to males more than females. Most candidates give the reason of "better prospects". This is wrong, as it implies that you are a money chaser rather than a career person. Should you happen to have several job moves in your resume, then you will need to think of a smart answer. A disagreeable superior is a bad reason to cite. It shows you cannot get along with your superiors. Domestic reasons are another wrong reason to quote. It shows that your personal life is interfering with your professional life. One good reply I received was, *"In my earlier years, I was not sure of what I wanted in terms of my career, hence the several job changes. I know now what I want and find that your organisation meets my aspirations"*. This explanation did not let his previous organisations down but, in fact, gave importance to the organisation he was applying for.

Integrity: This is evaluated through questions like, "What would you like to be—good or famous?" If your answer is "good", it indicates your priority to be law-abiding, honest, and fair. The answer "famous" may indicate, on the positive side, ambition and a desire to achieve, but on the negative side, it could also mean attaining fame at any cost. There was one candidate who gave an acceptable answer by saying, *"I could be good while achieving fame"*.

Teamwork: This is one quality valued in all organisations. Most interviewers must evaluate whether you are a team player. They are most likely going to pose a hypothetical question such as, "It is your day off, and a colleague asks you to come in and help clear the backlog of work. What would you do?" Obviously, you would like to help your team members out.

Attitude: Your attitude towards life would be important to an organisation. They could ask a question like, "If you won a lottery of a million, how would you spend it?" or "If you had a long weekend ahead, how would you spend it?" Most organisations would like a person who is purposeful and achievement-oriented. One good answer I received for the former question was, *"I will keep a large portion aside for my personal development by attending courses, which, as you know, are very expensive"*. I was personally impressed with the answer because it indicated to me that the candidate would always be on the quest for continuous improvement and education.

The second question on the weekend solicits how you value time. For heaven's sake, do not say that you will sleep or watch television the whole day. It shows an inert person who does not use time to move forward. One good answer I got was, "There is a self-improvement book I want to read and finish now that I have time". Another positive answer was, "I want to visit book stores to seek out a good book on leadership." It shows your zest for continuous improvement.

Risk-taking: This quality is evaluated by a hypothetical question like, "Suppose you had a choice to pick or not to pick one of two cards. One card will double the money in your wallet, while the other will confiscate whatever you have. What choice would you make?" Naturally, the one who picks a card is a risk-taker, whereas the one who does not plays safe is not. Is there a right or wrong? Not necessarily. It gives an input on your risk-taking ability.

9. **Presentations**

Interviewer's technique

Sometimes an interview will ask you to make a presentation on a subject. These are usually asked in middle management positions that require considerable communication skills with logic and knowledge. They will give you a case or topic and give you time to prepare and present. They want to see how you are able to communicate before a panel, your confidence, your communication skills, your depth of knowledge, your experience, and the logical way you put your ideas.

Your Tactic

Ask for what you may need for a presentation. It could be a laptop, in which case you can make your presentation using PowerPoint software. It would be most effective. Alternatively, you can ask for flip chart paper or a white board and pens. In such cases, you can use bullet points to guide you through. If either is not available, then use your notebook to pen down your salient points. You could keep the notebook open while presenting. Remember, diagrams speak better than words. So if you can represent your ideas through flow charts, it is more desirable. Use information that you know, not what you are sketchy about. It will give you confidence because of your familiarity with the contents.

10. **Closing an interview**

    Interviewer's technique

    An interviewer will indicate that the interview is concluded by several methods:

    1. He or she could ask a question: "I have nothing more to ask; do you have any questions?"
    2. The interviewer may close your file.
    3. The interviewer may stand up.
    4. The interviewer may say: "Thank you for coming for the interview; you shall hear from us shortly."

YOUR TACTIC

Make sure you have asked questions before the end of the interview. The types of questions to ask have been mentioned earlier. In the first option above, the interviewer gave you the chance to ask questions. This is a trained interviewer, but many may not be trained and may use the other options above. Insist on asking questions by simply saying, "May I take a little of your time to seek some clarifications that I have?" No interviewer will deny you this time. Be brief. It is better to list them in writing in a diary and read them out. An interviewer will appreciate the preparation you made to pen down questions. It also shows your interest in the organisation.

Seven

Types of Interviews and Selection Methods

INTERVIEWS

As mentioned earlier, an interview is an opportunity provided to you to be evaluated for selection and to evaluate whether the organisation is suitable for you. Organisations approach this task in many ways, with specific purposes and objectives. It is important to ascertain quickly what type of interview you are facing to be able to make a stance that fulfils the purpose of the interview. Some of these types of interviews are:

DIRECTED OR STRUCTURED INTERVIEWS

Most professional interviewers would use this type, especially when there is a time constraint and they have predetermined exactly what they want to know. The interviewer, very often, would have the questions or a checklist written in advance. Such interviews are impersonal and are based on soliciting facts. It leaves very little room to understand you as a person. You find this kind of approach adopted by employment bureaus, preliminary screening boards, or placement consultants at pre-screening stages. The approach for you is to have your facts ready, with certificates and testimonials ready to support them.

UNDIRECTED OR UNSTRUCTURED INTERVIEWS

This is the type of interview you will frequently face. Its purpose is to probe you thoroughly. This is achieved by the interviewer, who asks open-ended questions to encourage you to speak more. Normally, they will use these questions to clarify your resume further or to solicit information that is not found in your resume, such as your motivations, aspirations, personality traits, etc. Chapter 9, which shows frequently asked questions, gives you a taste of undirected interviews with probable answers.

PRELIMINARY INTERVIEW

A preliminary interview is one conducted initially, either in person or by phone, to determine whether you have the basic qualifications to warrant a subsequent interview. This is conducted usually by the HR department. The interview could be a combination of directed and undirected questions to gather facts and also to understand your personality, ambitions, and intentions. Such preliminary interviews could typically ask questions like:

1. Why do you wish to join our organisation?
2. What are your career goals?
3. What are your interests?
4. What are your strengths and weaknesses?

MULTIPLE INTERVIEWS

Multiple interviews follow the preliminary interview. It could be with several individuals who pool their findings or a panel of interviewers. In these interviews, the focus is on how you would perform the job in relation to the company's goals and objectives. A variation on this approach involves a series of interviews in which unsuitable candidates are screened out at each succeeding level of interviews.

PANEL INTERVIEWS

Panel interviews are popular to save time. Panel interviews include all those involved in the hiring decision. They meet together to question you from their respective perspectives, later discuss you, and give their decision there and then. A panel may have two to seven people.

Of all interviews, a panel interview can be the most stressful because you find yourself trying to sway several decision-makers rather than one or two. Unlike that old bit of advice, try to relate to each interviewer when s/he asks a question. It may sound difficult, but it is not impossible.

Your preparation would be the same as if it were for an individual interviewer, except that now the questions are asked by different people.

Remember that individuals like to hear their name during a conversation. It's important to know who is interviewing you, so ask their names and write them down within your notes—in order of where each is seated. Don't be afraid to use their names or ask questions throughout the process. Addressing them by name works like magic. Conversely, using the wrong names can backfire.

Another great technique to utilise within a panel interview or within any other group setting is to cross-reference the latest question with a previous one. For example, if you answer a question by Jane Doe and can incorporate that answer into another question asked by Frank Doe, you'll start navigating the outcome of the interview. An answer might be:

"I understand why you are asking a specific question about my social skills, Mr. Doe. As Ms. Jane asked a few minutes ago, social skills are critical to your success. To answer your question and expand upon what Ms. Jane asked earlier, I ..."

Do you see where I'm going with this? This answer is now important to two individuals on the panel rather than one. The key is to mark down concerns that are relevant to each interviewer. Although they are a team and have one common goal, each has differentiating concerns.

It's difficult to give enough eye contact to each individual without making your head and neck look like a lawn sprinkler. Try your best to look individuals in the eye and focus on speaking to each person equally, focusing heavily on the one who asked the question.

Unfortunately, a panel interview can be stressful for job seekers because they feel outnumbered. It's important to remember that you can be a possible asset to their business, and they obviously feel you're a viable candidate, or they wouldn't have scheduled the interview. Stay positive, remain calm, and answer each question thoroughly and effectively. Keep eye contact with everyone.

BOARD INTERVIEWS

Board interviews are normally held at the final selection stage or for senior appointments. The board consists of senior members of the organisation who bring collective experiences to ascertain your suitability for the culture and values of the organisation. The best way out is to recognise that you have reached this stage and that you matter to them. Treat each panel member as an individual and answer them one by one while sweeping your eyes over them periodically to include them in the discussion. It would be wonderful to know their individual names and use them when addressing them. It is important to keep calm and confident.

STRESS INTERVIEWS

This interview is used for stressful jobs. The interviewer wants to ascertain your ability to handle stress. You may be asked questions that make you uncomfortable. Although it is uncommon for an entire interview to be conducted under stressful conditions, it is common for the interviewer to incorporate stress questions as a part of a traditional interview. There are two types of stress: physical and emotional. Physical stress can be evaluated in physical group tasks. The emotional ones are tricky. There are ethical issues with the use of stress interviews. Candidates feel humiliated and cornered, bringing out sometimes unusual responses including anger, crying, blank outs, uncontrollable giggles, being sassy, etc. Be alert when asked such questions. Recognise that it is a stressful question. Be calm and even make light of the situation. Examples of stress questions are:

1. I don't like you. Convince me to start liking you.
2. I don't like the colour of your dress. Why did you wear it?
3. I don't think that women will be able to do this job. Why should we select you? (asked to a woman candidate)
4. You look nervous. Why are you so?

Caution for interviewers: There are several ethical and social issues involved, and it is best to avoid emotional stress during interviews.

SITUATIONAL INTERVIEWS

In this method, situations (caselets) are given of common problems you may encounter on the job. Your responses to these situations are measured against pre-determined standards. Some interviewers may even employ role-play, which is acting a situation out. One that I commonly used was asking a candidate to sell me a pen. I was the customer, and he was the salesperson. When presented with a situation like this, compose yourself. You may even pause to think and decide how you are going to approach it. There is no magic formula except to put yourself in the situation and imagine how you would approach it using your experience.

GROUP INTERVIEWS

Group interviews are used by selection panels for two reasons:

1. When there are too many candidates to interview on a given day, This method enables the interviewer(s) to assess large numbers of candidates and also saves time. This process takes place at the preliminary stages of a selection process.
2. To observe your behaviour in a group. This is important as organisations comprise large bodies of people working together towards a common objective. Interviewers want to see if you can work in a team.

It must be understood that group interviews are a part of the selection process and not an end in themselves. Group behaviour is only one part of an individual's total personality. Group interviews are taken essentially in three ways:

1. ***Group Discussion (GD)***

   A group of candidates will be asked to sit in a semi-circle or a full circle, with or without a table in between. The group will be given a topic for discussion. Most GDs have to discuss spontaneously. Sometimes interviewers give two to three topics for the group to choose from but assess how they go about choosing them. Once the topic is chosen, the group is given 15–30 minutes to discuss the topic. The interviewer observes the following:

2. **Role behaviour:** It is believed that when individuals are placed in undefined circumstances, they adopt roles that they are most comfortable with. The following roles emerge:

   * *Leader.* It is misconstrued that the leader is the one who talks the most. So each member of the group tries to out-talk the other, resulting sometimes in chaos. The leader is the one who initiates the discussion if the group is 'frozen'. If there is someone else who initiates the discussion, the leader is one who contributes to the discussion with quality and content. He or she is the one who offers various alternatives to the point of discussion. The leader is one who listens just as much as he or she contributes. One major role of the leader is to ensure that everyone gets a chance to speak. He or she will ensure the psychological and emotional health of the group and diffuse unhealthy disagreements. He or she finds solutions and alternatives to deadlocks. An important role of the leader is to keep track of time. He or she nudges the group forward and keeps the discussion flowing, especially when the group is spending too much time on a topic. The leader likes to arrive at a conclusion to offer to the interviewer(s) at the end of the debate. A leader is one who sets norms for the discussion, such as permitting everyone to speak or an agreement that a conclusion must be reached in a given time. The leader may even assign roles to everyone, such as time-keeping, noting down points, etc.

   * ***The challenger:*** He or she is a leader in a way by having the courage to disagree with the trend or point of discussion. He or she offers plausible arguments against the motion but tends to be rigid in his or her stance. S/he creates 'tension' in the group, therefore excitement and liveliness in the group. There is nothing wrong with this stance, provided the person is willing to listen and is able to get points across in a civil manner. There is a difference between assertion and aggression. Assertion is when you uphold a belief, while aggression is when you attack a personality. Assertion is preferred, and interviewers are quick to identify the two.

- *Active debater:* S/he is one who gets into the discussion almost immediately. She or he contributes to the strength of her confidence in people and his or her communication skills. She adds content to the discussion, and other debaters take stances for or against him or her. Such members are valued, provided they add content and quality to the discussion and do not speak for the sake of it. There are some who are excited and itching to be on the move. Such people are valued, provided they give others a chance to express their point of view. They sort of 'keep the ball rolling'.
- *Maintainers:* There are some who prefer to care for the health of the group. They try to diffuse heated arguments with wit and humour. They pacify members who are hurt by comments and stop those who are becoming aggressive. The leader takes on this role in the absence of a group health monitor.
- *Isolationist:* S/he is one who is overcome with the assertion and communication skills of other members. He or she would stay quiet for most of the discussion. It is not that he or she is not alert to the discussion. He or she may have some brilliant ideas but is just not getting the chance to enter the discussion. The leader is quick to notice this and draw the person out of the mainstream. Sometimes the isolationist may start parallel discussions outside of the mainstream because he or she is unable to get into the mainstream.

  We cannot say which role is right or wrong. It really depends on the position(s) for which selections are being held. Management positions obviously value leaders; debaters are preferred for jobs that involve public interfaces like customer service, public relations, sales and marketing, purchasing, etc. The health monitors may be suitable for human resource jobs, while the isolationists may be suitable for lonely jobs like research, accounting, IT, etc.

I. ***Communication skills:*** Another important outcome of a group discussion is proficiency in communications. A group discussion throws up an individual's ability to put forward ideas forcefully, articulately, and logically. Command over the language is essential for successful communication. The ability to listen and integrate other viewpoints with one's own is also assessed. Customer contact jobs may require better communication skills than back office ones. Leadership roles will require better communication skills than followers, who have to be good listeners.

2. ***Content:*** Very often, group members feel that it is the quantity of speaking that matters and not the quality of it. This is a misguided opinion. It is not how much you say, but what you say, that matters. The content is measured by your depth of knowledge and how logically and clearly it is put forward. Alternative viewpoints are always welcome to make the discussion richer. The interviewer must be 'stirred' by the discussion.

3. ***Emotional stability:*** Members in a group are under a bit of pressure, especially since all are aspiring to be selected. An immature group would build up this pressure by being inconsiderate of others. Some become argumentative, dogmatic, overbearing, biased, or emotionally aroused, while others become insecure, quiet, withdrawn, and nervous. Interviewers look for balanced individuals who are cool and composed yet assertive enough to hold their own.

SOME FAQS ABOUT GROUP DISCUSSIONS

Q1. Is it important for me to open the discussion?

A It is not necessary, though desirable. You will make an impact by opening the discussion only when the group is 'frozen'.

Q2. How much should I say?

A It is not how much you speak but the quality of your inputs. You may speak two or three times only, but if you are able to add new dimensions to the debate, it will be appreciated.

Q3. Which stance should I take?

A Be natural. You cannot be what you are not. The interviewer can tell when you are bluffing. Be conscious of the profile of the job and what qualities are best suited. Fulfil those in the group discussion.

Q4. *What if I do not get a chance to speak?*

A Assert yourself by saying, "Excuse me, I have something to contribute." The interviewers will see whether other group members will let you contribute. It works against them if they do not let you do so.

Q5. *Where should I sit in the discussion room?*

The seating in a group discussion plays an important role. Some seating is pre-assigned, while others allow the group members to choose their seating. Let us see how seating makes a difference in a group discussion using the diagram below:

We will see that the most influential position in the seating is C. By sheer fortune, position C can assume leadership because the tendency is to look to the centre. If you are positioned there, then take advantage of asserting yourself in leadership. Positions B and D normally support the leader C in arguments and act as 'henchmen'. The positions A, E, F, and K act as cornerstones to the structure and may most possibly take on the maintainer role of keeping group harmony. The positions H and M tend to become the challengers as they assume leadership positions because they are the centres of the limbs. The dotted lines show their opposition to leader C, and they may try to even ignore C. The positions G, I, L, and M act as 'henchmen' to the challengers and are the activists of their cause, as represented by broken lines. There may be heated debate between the two limbs because the two limbs face each other in opposition. The leader will have to keep the fierce debate between the two in check. The positions in J and O are unfortunate and may get isolated. The isolationists need to beware of being cut off from the debate if their natural tendency is non-assertive. These two positions may start their own discussions because they are out of the main stream. The leader will have to make a special effort to bring them into the discussion.

It is good to know the power or handicap of positions to make that special effort to promote your own natural tendencies. So if active debaters are put in positions J and O, they will have to assert themselves more to be in the discussion. Similarly, if challengers are 'cornered' in positions A, E, F, and K, they will have to make a special effort to gather support for their ideas and influence the leader. A leader will find it difficult to manage the group if seated in any other position.

Q6. ***What if I know nothing about the topic?***

1. Listen to the discussion and understand it. You can support one of the arguments by saying, "I agree with this point," and you may even repeat a point. It is indeed unfortunate if you do not understand the subject.

Q7. ***What if I have poor communication skills?***

1. Tough luck! It will work against you. The best you can do is agree or disagree by summarising points already stated.

Q8. ***Is there a sure way of knowing if I have done well?***

1. No! Many candidates who spoke a lot felt they had done well only to be rejected. Remember, quality, not quantity, is important.

Some popular topics for discussion are:

1. Russia's war on Ukraine, justified or not.
2. Role of the UN in peacekeeping
3. Position of women in India compared to other nations.
4. How do you make our environment sustainable?
5. Is China better than India in manufacturing?
6. BPOs in India: A success or failure?
7. What has Bharat done to achieve world dominance?
8. Is digital marketing ruining viewing pleasure?
9. Is China a threat to India?
10. Bharat or the West, which is the land of opportunities?
11. Should water resources be nationalised?

12. How can we maintain a balance between a career and the family?
13. What is the effect of mobile devices on youth?
14. Compare the education in India to that in foreign nations.
15. Is it necessary to ban Coca-Cola in India?
16. Are studies more beneficial in India or abroad?
17. Are women taking over the workplace?
18. America's war on terrorism: success or failure?
19. Climate change—whose responsibility is it?
20. Women's march from bedroom to boardroom
21. The future of Africa
22. War on Poverty
23. How can we bring back hockey's past glory in India?
24. India's failure in the cricket World Cup—what went wrong?
25. Should Bharat be a military superpower?
26. The present state of the Indian cricket team
27. Love marriage vs. arranged marriage
28. What are the advantages and disadvantages of co-education?

HOT TOPICS:

1. How do we deal with international terrorism?
2. Should we pursue our policy of dialogue with Pakistan?
3. Are peace and non-violence outdated concepts?

GROUP TASK

This is a selection process where a group of 5–10 participants is given a physical task to accomplish. The task has several hurdles that require leaping, twisting, swinging, etc. to test physical prowess. This method is used by military selection boards but is increasingly used by other commercial ventures that require outdoor physical prowess, such as oil rigs, adventure sports organisation, etc. Human skills involve working as a team as well as leadership qualities like encouragement during failure, recognition of success, assisting members who are falling short of expectations, allotting responsibilities, and setting personal examples. Physical abilities include endurance, stamina, coordination of the body, etc.

While the above is usually performed outdoors, there are group tasks performed indoors. Groups are pitched against each other to complete a task that requires teamwork and intergroup coordination. Interviewers evaluate your behaviour in a team as well as your interaction with other groups. Within the group, members naturally adopt natural roles such as the *leader*, who provides the plan, strategy, and direction; the *negotiator*, who is comfortable interacting with other groups and negotiating for resources; the maintainer, who looks after the psychological and emotional health of the group by managing differences within the group, especially when they are under pressure or in crisis; the worker, who is comfortable with industry and manual effort to complete the task; the loner, who waits to be invited to take part in the discussion or is totally disinterested in the group's effort; and an effort philosopher, who gives ideas and creative ways of looking at the task.

The interviewer also sees the interaction with other groups, whether they are cooperative or selfish, trusting or suspicious, fighting or sabotaging, taking pride in the group, or bringing them down. There are many other assessments interviewers can make.

DIALOGUE PANEL

In this instance, the discussion is between the candidates and the interviewer, who skilfully brings out the personal qualities, attitudes, and motivations of the candidates through clever questions. In this method, the interviewer ensures that everyone gets a chance to speak. The topic could be any topical issue. In such selection processes, there are certain golden rules to follow:

1. Be involved and participative in the discussion.
2. Give qualitative input.

3. Listen carefully to what others are saying because you may be asked by the interviewer to respond to it.
4. Be cool and composed. Do not lose your cool or get into an argument.
5. Be assertive, not aggressive.
6. Be natural—don't act.
7. Sit with an upright posture.
8. Don't be excitable, but be composed in your deliberations.

CASE STUDIES

What is a case question?

A case question is a fun, interactive interviewing tool used to evaluate the multi-dimensional aspects of a candidate. You and others are presented with real-life information and asked to analyse, synthesize, and articulate a solution.

What is the purpose of the case question?

Interviewers use case questions to see how well candidates listen, how they think, the logic behind their thoughts, and how well they can articulate their thoughts under pressure. Consulting firms also ask case questions to gauge self-confidence, discover the candidate's personality, and see if problem solving genuinely intrigues them.

What's the objective of a case question?

The objective is not to determine if the interviewee got the "right answer," but rather to evaluate the process the candidate used to structure a competent approach to derive a solution. They test how you:

1. analyse information
2. sort through an excess of data and identify the main points
3. think logically, structure their thought process, and organise their answer.
4. maintain poise and clearly communicate under pressure.

5. display personality and characteristics that are considered a good "fit" with the company.

They are looking to see if the candidates are:

- Relaxed, confident, and mature?
- Engaging and enthusiastic?
- Good listeners?
- Able to determine what is truly relevant?
- Asking insightful and probing questions
- Organising the information effectively and developing a logical framework for analysis?
- Stating assumptions clearly
- Approaching the case creatively
- Comfortable discussing the multifunctional aspects of the case?
- Trying to quantify their response at every opportunity?
- Displaying both business sense and common sense?
- Exhibiting strong social and presentation skills

Are all cases verbal, or do some firms ask for written cases?

While most cases are written, some firms give a verbal case. The candidate is given 30 to 45 minutes to read the case and make notes. He or she is then questioned about the case.

Sometimes this is done one-on-one, other times the candidate is brought in as part of a group to solve the case. This is done to see how well a candidate can work as part of a team with strangers. Is the candidate trying to dominate the interview, or is she building on what another candidate said? Is she communicating laterally as well as vertically?

TIPS FOR HANDLING CASES

- Identify the problem.
- Make notes of key points if the case is read out to you.

- Read the case carefully and underline those points that have a bearing on the question.
- Ask for clarifications.
- Make assumptions about your arguments.

WHAT INTERVIEWERS ARE OBSERVING WHILE STUDYING THE CASE

- Have you identified the problem?
- Are you writing down the case information?
- Have you clarified questions about the company, the industry, the competition, and the product?
- Are you laying out a logical structure for their answer with data?

What do interviewers observe during the discussion?

- Are you enthusiastic, and do you project a positive attitude?
- Are you logical and making good business sense?
- Is your answer well-organised?
- Did you state your assumptions clearly?
- Are you creative?
- Are you engaging and bringing others into the conversation?
- Are you asking probing questions?
- Are you quantifying your answer as much as possible?
- Are you listening to others?
- Are you bogged down in details?
- Have you gone off-tangent?
- Did you use buzz words and business terms correctly?
- Did you have trouble with math, percentages, etc.?
- Did you summarise the answer?
- Were you assertive or aggressive?

- Did you keep to the time limits set?

Handling verbal case questions

- Keep a note book and a pen or pencil at hand to note key points of the case and the question. Repeat it back to be clear.
- Think before you answer. Don't jump off the mark and give the first answer that pops into your head. Take your time and analyse the information.
- Ask for numbers. It will help you quantify your answers. If the numbers aren't an important part of the case, they will more than likely tell you not to focus on them.
- Prioritise and then address the issues one at a time; your interviewer may not expect you to get through all of them in the allotted time.
- Turn the interview into a conversation. A five-minute monologue will do more to hurt your chances than any other mistake. Remember, you ask questions not only to get additional information but also to draw the interviewer into the case with you.
- If you are getting lost during your answer, stop and summarise what you said so far. This will lift you out of the mud of details and hopefully show you a new path to take.
- Keep track of the time. You must reach a conclusion.
- Remember that there is no right or wrong answer. It is your process of arriving at your answer that matters.

THE 12 MOST POPULAR CASE SCENARIOS

Business cases have traditionally focused on either business strategy or business operations. However, with today's more complex cases, candidates are getting cases that cover both categories and multiple scenarios.

Strategy Scenarios	Operating Scenarios
Entering a new market	Increasing sales
Developing a new product	Reducing Costs

Pricing Strategies	Improving the bottom line
Growth Strategies	Turnarounds
Mergers & Acquisitions	
Starting a new business	
Competitive response Industry Analysis	

BEHAVIOURAL INTERVIEWS

Behavioural interviews reveal how you acted in specific employment-related situations in the past. The logic is that your past behaviour will predict your future behaviour in similar situations, i.e., past performance predicts future performance.

TRADITIONAL INTERVIEW VS. BEHAVIOURAL INTERVIEW

In a traditional interview, you will be asked a series of questions that typically have straight-forward answers, like "What are your strengths and weaknesses?" or "What major challenges and problems did you face? How did you handle them?" or "Describe a typical work week."

In a behavioural interview, an employer has decided what skills are needed in the person they hire and will ask questions to find out if the candidate has those skills. Behavioural interview questions will be more pointed, probing, and specific than traditional interview questions.

- Give an example of an occasion when you used logic to solve a problem.
- Give an example of a goal you reached and tell me how you achieved it.
- Describe a decision you made that was unpopular and how you handled implementing it.
- Have you gone above and beyond the call of duty? If so, how?
- What do you do when your schedule is interrupted? Give an example of how you handled it.

* Have you had to convince a team to work on a project they weren't thrilled about? How did you do it?
* Have you handled a difficult situation with a co-worker? How?
* Tell me about how you worked effectively under pressure.

Follow-up questions will also be detailed. You may be asked what you did, what you said, how you reacted, or how you felt.

Preparation for the Potential Behavioural Interview

Remember that you won't know what type of interview will take place until you are sitting in the interview room. So, prepare answers to traditional interview questions.

Then, since you don't know exactly what situations you will be asked about if it's a behavioural interview, refresh your memory and consider some special situations you have dealt with or projects you have worked on. You may be able to use them to help frame responses. Prepare stories that illustrate times when you have successfully solved problems or performed memorably. The stories will be useful to help you respond meaningfully in a behavioural interview.

Finally, review the job description, if you have it, or the job posting or ad. You may be able to get a sense of what skills and behavioural characteristics the employer is seeking from reading the job description and position requirements. Recall some situations in your experience that brought out those behaviours.

During the Behavioural interview

During the interview, if you are not sure how to answer the question, ask for clarification. Then be sure to include these points in your answer:

* A specific situation
* The tasks that are needed to be done
* The action you took
* The results, i.e., what happened

It's important to keep in mind that there are no right or wrong answers. The interviewer is simply trying to understand how you behaved in a given situation. How you respond will determine if there is a fit between your skills and the position the company is seeking to fill. So, listen carefully, be clear and detailed when you respond, and, most importantly, be honest. If your answers aren't what the interviewer is looking for, this position may not be the best job for you anyway.

VIDEO INTERVIEW

Video interviews are done when the distances between the interviewer and interviewee are great. It is cheaper and does not involve the cost of air or train tickets. A video interview may seem simpler and less stressful than a face-to-face one, but it isn't.

Video interviews are face-to-face occasions and deserve all the preparations of a physical meeting. A video interview may be a precursor to a physical face-to-face interview.

It's important to recognise why video interviews are becoming popular. Time is one of the biggest factors. As interviewers take on more responsibilities, they're trying to find time-saving techniques to fit into their busy schedules. The interviewer can discuss matters prior to an official meeting, clarify discrepancies or concerns, conduct an informal introduction, discuss the position, and/or ask for additional career information.

The interview is normally scheduled in advance. You could have a "cheat sheet" next to your computer for facts, dates, and important issues. You'll want to have a resume on hand that you can refer to as well as a notepad so that you can write down information that is given to you by your interviewer.

Without an outline or list of potential answers, these types of discussions (interviews) can get casual. A casual phone interview can provoke unrelated and untargeted answers.

Create an outline that might resemble this:

Specific skills (broken down)

Position and industry

Specific Accomplishments

Successful cost-cutting measures

Unique Assets as an Employee

(e.g., language skills, cutting-edge technology, techniques)

There are some specific things that you can do to make sure that you score well in the video interview. The first thing that you need to do is dress formally as though you were going for a physical interview. The interviewer could well ask you to get up and see your full profile. Eliminate distractions that can occur while you're on the video call. Tell the family not to disturb you.

Distractions include subtle noises such as your dog barking, your cell phone ringing, or someone in the background who is doing the dishes. Try to schedule your phone interview in a quiet place so that you don't have to fight against distractions. You need to be as focused as you can be so that you can concentrate on the answers to the questions that you're asked. Avoid slang and speak like a professional. Smile throughout.

Luncheon Interviews

There may be times when your job interview is conducted over lunch or coffee. This is because many employers have busy schedules, and they will try to kill two birds with one stone: a meal and your interview. There are some interviews that will be held at breakfast with one interviewer, followed by lunch with another, and then dinner with yet another.

One of the reasons why many employers will conduct a meal interview is because they want to see you in a variety of social settings, particularly if this is something that is part of your job description and you'll be required to meet with clients on a regular basis (e.g., sales, public relations, etc.). No matter what the reason is for the meal interview, you need to prepare as you would for a regular interview.

A luncheon interview has some benefits. The relaxed setting can provide casual interaction. This type of meeting can be informative. Here are a few tips for you at such meetings:

Dress. Dress formally as though you were attending an office interview. Though the setting is informal, the occasion is formal.

Be on time. Make sure that you agree to a venue known to you. If the interviewer has already made the choice, make sure you get directions to the venue, if it is not known to you. Plan to be early by at least ten minutes. It is important that you wait for the interviewer, not the other way around. Inform the restaurant hostess where you are seated or ask for the table reserved for the interviewer. Leave your name with them. If nothing else, wait in the foyer.

Seating. Wait for your interviewer to sit down before you do. This shows respect and courtesy and will leave a lasting impression that is positive. Your interviewer wants to see how you conduct yourself in a social setting, so take the opportunity to show off your best professionalism. Sit up straight while keeping your feet flat on the floor. Crossing your legs can come across as too casual.

Be confident. It can be nerve-wracking when someone watches you eat. Actually, a person's confidence level can be determined by how poised they are. A confident eater will eat with poise and correctness, while a nervous one will not be able to concentrate on anything else. Your social etiquette is noticed, especially for jobs where you have to entertain clients.

Manage your food. Unfold your napkin. Order the least expensive item on the menu. Again, this is all about common courtesy, and your interviewer just wants to see how you handle yourself in this type of situation. Choose items that are easily manageable. Lamb chops will need deft slicing just like a chicken piece. A salad is easily managed. Handle your food carefully. Practice beforehand, if necessary. You will certainly make a bad impression if you can't handle your own food: Simple rules to follow:

- Break bread into small and manageable bites.
- Avoid anything that can spill.
- Don't suggest or order alcoholic beverages (even if the interviewer does).
- Order something similar to your interviewer.

- Use your napkin to wipe your mouth and disguise picking teeth (or visit the restroom).
- Never use fingers unless the meal consists of a sandwich or finger food.

Eat slowly by taking small bites. You'll most likely be asked questions while you're eating, and you want to be able to answer without food spitting out of your mouth or choking on large pieces. Keep your arms off the table and remember to use the correct cutlery as dictated by what you're eating. Remember the purpose of your meal: this is a job interview, and you want to do the best that you can so that you get the job or move on to the second round of interviews.

Thank the interviewer. As with any interview, thank everyone present with a firm handshake. Approximately 70% of interviewees do not send a thank-you letter after the meeting, so set yourself apart from the rest. **SEND A TEXT MESSAGE!**

APTITUDE TESTS

Aptitude tests reflect the hierarchical structure of your intelligence in relation to an average worker. Aptitude tests are composed of numerical, verbal, and spatial ability scales brought together as a test battery. They can then be scored and interpreted individually as a specific ability or aptitude measure or together as part of a general ability measure. You cannot bluff these tests. Be natural. Aptitude tests are only one of the inputs in a selection process. They are never an end in themselves. They actually measure your abilities and talents using the four criteria mentioned above. So an accountant must be high in numeric ability; a salesperson must be good at verbal ability; and an ad man must be good at spatial ability. Aptitude tests are usually administered at entry-level jobs and trainee positions.

PERSONALITY TESTING

Personality is a term that is commonly used in everyday language but that has been given a particular technical meaning by psychologists. When we discuss personality, we must remember that it is not a single independent mechanism but is closely related to other human cognitive and emotional systems. There are many personality tests for different levels of jobs that can bring out aspects of leadership, team spirit, emotional make-up under stress, etc.

Eight

Profiles of Interviewers

I am sure that most of you would like to know what interviewers are like. Interviewers differ in that they have different values, cultural backgrounds, and thought processes. It is difficult to cover all these characteristics, but I have simplified this complex process by grouping them into a few styles. Whatever their style, their intention is the same: *to get the right person for the job.* Their styles vary because not all are trained interviewers. Many interviewers are line managers or have functions other than human resources. Human resource professionals are expected to be trained interviewers. Before we see the various styles that untrained interviewers adopt, let us see what a trained interviewer will be like:

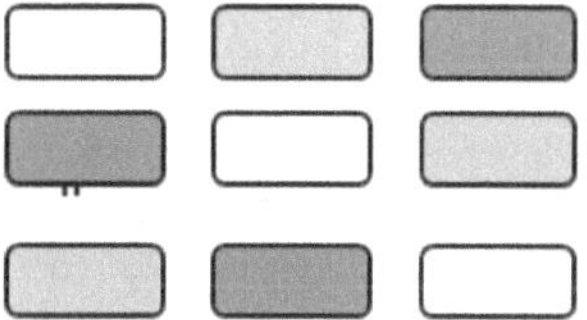

1. S/he is acutely aware of being a representative of the organisation and also takes care in grooming well for the interview. He or she chooses a pleasant environment for the interview and also speaks politely to the candidate. He or she makes sure that he or she is in time for the interview.

2. She or he strives to improve her interviewing skills continuously. He or she will look upon every interview as a learning opportunity and will try new techniques and methods to improve. Be aware that you could be teaching her something too.

3. He or she learns from candidates, new concepts, and ideas and evaluates whether they can be used in his or her own organisation.

4. He or she prepares for the interview. S/he reviews the resume thoroughly and notes down questions or clarifications that do not reflect in the resume.

5. He or she upgrades himself or herself on the job subject so as not to look stupid at the interview.

6. S/he is well informed on the legal aspects of the job being offered, as well as questions she can and cannot ask in an interview.

7. She or he uses an interview rating form to record her comments about you for other decision-makers to see.

8. He or she believes in the 80:20 principle, where the candidate speaks 80% of the time.

9. He or she will put the candidate at ease with the belief that a relaxed candidate will be able to perform better at the interview and will be more forthcoming with information. He or she will make gestures like offering you water or coffee.

10. He or she believes that experience is more important than academic qualifications. He or she is willing to accept theoretical principles, provided their linkage is demonstrated to real-life situations.

11. While s/he feels secure writing down the positive qualities of a candidate, s/he is cautious of writing down negative ones unless absolutely sure. He or she makes sure by artfully asking other questions to confirm a negative point. He or she would prefer to discuss negative points further with other interview members before recording negative comments. This may come as a relief to candidates because they have to consistently show a negative quality during the interview to warrant it being written down.

12. He or she wants to be in control of the interview and alter its direction whenever it is convenient.

13. He or she feels uncomfortable telling a candidate that he or she has been rejected. He or she takes into account your feelings of hurt and disappointment. He or she prefers to send a letter of rejection.

Most candidates may be unaware of the characteristics above. Knowledge of this will give some insight into the process of the interview.

More important is the fact that the interviewer is not an omnipotent person but a normal human being.

There are however many interviewers who are not trained and seem to possess a dominant style during the interview. You should be prepared for them too and know how to deal with them.

THE BRAGGART

The Braggart loves talking about his own achievements and experiences. He is basically insecure and has an overwhelming need to prove his self-worth. You become his 'captive audience'. You can best respond by admiring his achievements. The more you 'applaud' him, the better are his chances of being selected. He learns very little about you. It is best to listen to him and wait for those moments to offer something about yourself with connecting statements like, "I had a similar experience" or "I can see what you mean. In my experience..."

THE PERSECUTOR

He is a person who perhaps is persecuted by others within the organisation and looks at you as his whipping board. He asks questions that perhaps cannot be answered. He prides himself on humiliating you. It is unfortunate if you come across such an individual. Humility is the best stance to take, to the point where he feels satisfied pitying you. You can offer what you want him to know through a suggestion but be prepared to have your suggestion vetoed. Speak with confidence. He perhaps wants to see if you will resist his pressure. Do not argue.

THE DREAMER

He is the one who will let you talk as much as you want. He is perhaps not listening and is distracted by something else. He may not even maintain eye contact. Do not be despondent. He has probably trained his mind to concentrate on two things. He may be signing papers or shuffling them, but he is quite alert to what you are saying. He will interject only when necessary. Respond by telling him as much as you can about yourself, your achievements, and your experiences. You will have to "sell" yourself to make an impression on him. Vary your tone or speed to grab his attention. Even humour works.

THE PROFESSOR

He has such a patronising air that he knows it all. He gives those supercilious smiles that have a discomforting effect on you. His questions will be perfect and mostly bookish. He would like to end the interview by giving advice and counsel. Humility works well with him. Show interest in his advice and acknowledge that it is the best you have ever gotten.

THE PROGRAMMER

He approaches the interview as though it were a programme with a definite schedule. He has decided precisely what he wants to know and would have, more often than not, written down his questions. He asks them in sequence. It is best to answer him to the point and lucidly. He would like the answers in a logical form; therefore, it is best to give answers in a point-wise fashion.

THE FRIEND

He has a very open and casual style. The interview gets very personal, and he reveals a lot of himself and expects you to do so too. He is more concerned with your personal qualities than your work experience. In such circumstances, play along with his mood, but punctuate the joviality with something positive about yourself and your achievements. Do not mistake his informality for being too casual yourself. Be professional. Sometimes the friend can con you into revealing things that you would normally not do in an interview.

THE HARASSED

He is one person who is not organised. He does not brief his secretary to hold all phone calls. He answers them during the interview, which spoils the rhythm of the interview. He will also be distracted by issuing instructions or issuing a memo. You may have to repeat yourself after the distraction with sentences like, "As I was saying..." He will apologise for the interruptions all the time with the explanation that he is very busy. He may revive the interview by saying, "Where were we?" He may ask you questions, but his mind is elsewhere. It would be quiet in order to seek another time if he was busy. This would also be a hint to him that he is not respecting your time. In all probability, he will then concentrate on you.

Whatever the style adopted by the interviewer, keep a professional image. Your objective is to sell yourself. That can be done by recognising and adapting to his style. Concentrate on the questions, not the style the interviewer adopts.

Nine

101 Frequently Asked Interview Questions and Answers

After years of interviewing for various positions, either alone, with another person, or with a panel, I have found certain questions that arise very often. These questions are relevant to everyone. In this section, I wish to present some typical questions and how to approach them.

Interviews with the HR Manager

The HR Manager will typically be the first contact with you with the purpose of clarifying the following:

1. Facts in the resume
2. Your motivations
3. Your aspirations
4. Your personality traits
5. Your strengths and weaknesses
6. Your long-term goals

Interviews with the direct supervisor or manager

The interviews with the direct supervisor, manager, or panel are more concerned with the technical aspects of the job. Their questions would typically determine the following:

1. Your technical proficiency
2. Nature of your experience
3. Your performance record
4. Your achievements in past jobs
5. Your job fits
6. How do you fit into the functional team?
7. Your leadership style (for supervisory positions)
8. Ability to work under pressure, stress, or difficulty
9. Your work habits
10. Your specific job motivations
11. Your personality traits are specific to the job.
12. Customer orientation (if the job requires it)
13. Ability to work with the immediate superior
14. Salesmanship (if the job requires it)
15. Your creativity and innovation
16. The new ideas and experience you bring to the job

Final interview

The final interview would include all top management, but most probably the CEO/owner, functional head, and HR manager. They would be concerned with the following:

1. The culture fits the organisation.
2. The real commitment to the new company
3. Future potential
4. Flexibility in job positioning
5. Honesty, loyalty, and sincerity

6. Ability to look at 'the big picture'
7. Image as a representative of the company
8. Whether the organisation can fulfil your short- and long-term aspirations
9. Result orientation

The above objectives are in broad terms. It does not mean they cannot be included in various interview stages. The matter of salary is treated separately as it is discussed at the last stage, usually when the candidate is found fit for the organisation.

Here are 101 frequently asked questions (FAQs) for you to prepare for your interviews:

HR INTERVIEW QUESTIONS

Q1. "Tell me about yourself."

Unfortunately, most candidates already recount their resume in front of the interviewer, which is boring to the interviewer. This is the opportunity to sell yourself by stating what is not in your resume, such as your strengths, special qualities, achievements, aspirations, motivations, and ambitions. The more you say, the greater the opportunity to impress.

Many candidates feel awkward talking about themselves, preferring to be humble. The interview is the only occasion where you are licensed to talk about yourself in glowing terms. The interviewers expect it. This question requires preparation. You can even list it down and refer to it at the interview.

Q2. I have not had time to read your resume. Tell me about yourself.

This is a similar question to the one above, but this time you have to detail out your resume as well. You can follow the directions given below:

1. *Educational qualification*
2. *Work Experiences*

3. *Achievements and Honours*
4. *Why are you here?* Your aspirations, growth goals, etc.

Q3. What are your interests?

This could well be one of the earliest questions to make you feel comfortable with a familiar topic. As mentioned earlier, you would have listed your hobbies and interests in the resume, even if it was just one. The interviewer's belief is that if a person who has a hobby or interest is thorough about it, s/he is most likely to be thorough about the job s/he chooses. Caution: Please do not mention watching television or movies or texting on your mobile. Unfortunately, millennials do not have serious hobbies. Mention your interests then, like geopolitics, fashion, biographies, novels, sports, etc. Know everything about it.

The interviewer judges your **commitment** to your hobby or interest.

Q4. "Which were the high points of your school and college?"

This question is often asked of those entering the job market. Interviewers see your **achievement orientation** in your academics and extracurricular activities. As an interviewer, I had disdain for those who had no achievements. It gave me the impression that the candidate would be another passenger in the organisation. Some notable high points in school and college could be awards in academics, sports, leadership roles, and representation of the educational institution in public forums and competitions.

Q5. "What are your strengths and weaknesses?"

This question has stumped many candidates in my experience. An interviewer works on the belief that a person who knows himself or herself is more likely to be effective in life. Candidates find it difficult to verbalise their strengths and weaknesses because of a lack of preparation. Others find it difficult to mention weaknesses for fear of being rejected. Mention those strengths and weaknesses that will lend support to the job you are applying for. Here are some examples:

Strengths: hardworking, committed, achievement-oriented, strong in communication skills, team person, detailed in execution, quality conscious, loyal, honest, etc.

Weaknesses can be so crafted as to actually turn out to be strengths in certain circumstances, such as being a perfectionist, ethically ambitious, working till the job is complete, intolerant of dishonesty, slow at times to ensure safety and quality, needing time off to continuously upgrade myself, etc.

You can have an alternate strategy to this question by describing what you like most and like least, making sure that what you like most matches up with the most important qualification for success in the position and what you like least is not essential to the job position.

Example: Let's say you're applying for a sales position.

"If given a choice, I like to spend as much time as possible in front of my prospects selling, as opposed to shuffling paperwork back at the office".

This would be music to the interviewer's ears if he were the sales manager.

Q6. Do you have any regrets about your job?

This is an artfully framed question that seeks to bring out your weaknesses. You may bring out non-consequential regrets or use your own tactic to answer the question. Pause as though it never occurred to you, then say,

"As a general principle, I've found that the best way to avoid regrets is to avoid causing them in the first place. As a practice, at the end of each day, I mentally review the day's events and conversations to evaluate whether I will have any regrets. I immediately rectify them before regret occurs".

Q7. "Why do you want to leave your present job?"

This question is asked to ascertain your loyalty and future plans. Never let down your organisation or the people you work for. Some of the reasons you can give are:

proximity of the workplace to your residence; the new job fulfils your career objectives; you need career growth; you are ready for a larger responsibility; you want to join a larger company; the new job is a greater match for your skills and experience; etc.

If you are headhunted (targeted for recruitment by competition) and not yet 100% committed to leaving your present post, don't be afraid to say so. It shows your strong loyalty to your present job. Since you have a job, you are in a stronger position than someone who does not. But don't be coy, either. State honestly what you'd be hoping to find in a new job. Articulate your aspirations in terms of job title, higher responsibilities, salary, and a career path to grow further.

Q8. Why aren't you presently employed?

This is a tricky question, as it lowers your bargaining power. Organisations like to hire those with a consistent work record and those presently employed. One possible reason is that you were fired from your previous job. Never lie about having been fired. It's unethical and too easily checked. Deflect the reason from you personally to other reasons, such as:

Management takeover, merger, division-wide layoff, downsizing, etc.

You can also say, "*I felt it was unethical to apply for another job, so I resigned.*"

or

"*I found that while working, I was too busy to look for ideal opportunities for myself. Now, with free time, I am able to evaluate each organisation better so that I can have a long time with the organisation I finally choose*".

Another good reason could be that you were going back to study to improve your qualifications. Make sure that you are enrolled in a course!

Q9. "Why do you want to leave your present job so soon?"

This question is asked if you have recently joined an organisation and want to leave it. An interviewer is suspicious of someone who changes jobs so quickly. It forebodes a possible job-hopper, or you are not loyal to any organisation; or you do not know what you want; or you were found unsuitable during the probationary period; or you did not get along with your boss, etc. You will have to give a really good reason. Some acceptable reasons could be:

1. *The job was not as it was described.*
2. *The organisation changed its focus and goals*
3. *mismatch with your talents and skills*
4. *Change in management: wanted to bring in own staff*
5. *Downsizing, reorganisation*
6. *Hired for a short-term project*

Circumstances also come into play. Your ideal job was not readily available, and you took your present job to gain some experience. Emphasise that that the job you have now applied for is your dream job. If you have held other jobs for substantial periods and took the other job in good faith, stress your past performance. You are not a job hopper. You have skills to offer and want to put them to good use.

Q10. "What are your short- and long-term goals?"

The question is aimed at ascertaining your aspirations. Mention your aspirations over a five-year period. Anytime more will be just dreams. You are allowed to dream.

The interviewer ascertains how you have goals that mesh with the organisations. I feel I must continue to learn, to grow into a position of more responsibility, and to have made a significant contribution to the organisation."

Examples of good responses include:

* *"My long-term goals involve growing with a company where I can continue to learn, take on additional responsibilities, and contribute as much value as I can".*
* *"I see myself as a top-performing employee in a well-established organisation, like this one. I plan on enhancing my skills and continuing my involvement in (related) professional associations".*

* *"Once I gain additional experience and learning, I would like to move on from a technical position to management".*

Q11. "Why did you choose this particular field of work?"

This question is asked to get to know your temperament, attitudes, and personal qualities and how they relate to the job. The perfect match brings about commitment. For example, an accountant may like to be detailed, patient, sit at the workplace for many hours, be good with figures, find challenges in numeric problems, etc. A salesperson, on the other hand, is an extrovert, likes pleasing people, finds negotiation a challenge, is energetic, loves travel, likes to dress well, finds achieving sales targets exciting, etc.

Q12. Looking back, what would you do differently in your career?

This question could well be a trap for the earlier question. It is asked to confirm your commitment to what you are presently doing. It also wants to find out whether you celebrate life or whether you are a moaner.

Indicate that you are a happy, fulfilled, and optimistic person and that, in general, you wouldn't change a thing. For example, you could say:

"It's been a good life, rich in learning and experience, and the best is yet to come. Every experience in life is a lesson in its own way. I wouldn't change a thing, including my profession."

Q13. What do you worry about?

Redefine the word 'worry' so that it does not reflect negatively on you. Example:

"I wouldn't call it worry, but I am a strongly goal-oriented person. So I keep turning over in my mind anything that seems to be keeping me from achieving those goals until I find a solution. That's part of my tenacity, I suppose".

Q14. What makes you angry?

Give an answer that will uplift your personality and your style. To answer this, you would have already done some homework and be prepared.

Some reasons that look good in an interview are:

- When people tell lies
- When people are not meeting deadlines
- When people do not achieve your high standards
- When people do not show humility
- When situations are unfair
- When bosses rebuke in public
- When subordinates are not cost-conscious
- When people are habitually absent from work

You will see that your personality traits are highlighted. In other words, you are honest, meet deadlines, have high standards, are humble, fair, uphold people's self-respect, are cost-conscious, and are punctual. Wow! I would love to have such a person.

Q15. "What makes you tick?"

This is a wonderful open question to promote yourself as best as you can. It wants to know what motivates you. Some good motivational spurs are: challenge, innovation, solving problems, achieving result-oriented goals, working well with a team, higher responsibilities, working against targets, etc. Choose one or more that can lend itself to the job at hand.

Q16. Why aren't you earning more money at this stage of your career?

There can be many reasons why you are not making more money.

- You were in the learning mode when experience was more important than money.
- You preferred to work for a professional company that paid less than an unprofessional one that paid more.
- You respected the company values, which were more important than money.
- There were tremendous growth opportunities in the future.

- You prefer to work for a stable company.
- The quality of work-life was better at the companies where you worked.
- You wanted to work for a company with a reputed brand name.
- You preferred the perfect job fit to motivate you.

The interviewer must not see you as a dollar chaser but as someone who is well-rounded. Here is one good answer I received to the question:

"I guess everyone has their own ballpark as to what is enough for them. What I earn is enough for my needs. I would rather concentrate on a better job where I can perform better and earn more money through performance than get good money and be miserable."

Q17. Who has inspired you in your life, and why?

This is a wonderful question to evaluate your own benchmarks. Have a few heroes in mind with qualities of good professionalism. Industry leaders may add to your professional image. There is nothing wrong with mentioning sports stars, musicians, or philanthropists, as long as you can highlight the special qualities you admire. Relate them to your performance and attitudes. Some laudable qualities you can work around are:

- Excellence
- Perfection
- Humility
- Consistency
- Compassion
- Achievement oriented
- Concern for others
- Reliability

Q18. "What sport do you prefer?"

This question is asked for several reasons:

- Whether you are active or passive, Those who participate in sports are considered more physically active than those with sedentary pursuits like reading, painting, etc.
- It elicits whether you prefer individual sports or team sports. Individual sports are tennis, swimming, badminton, golf, etc., while team sports are those like football, hockey, cricket, etc. Those in team sports are more likely to understand teamwork to attain goals, while individuals in individual sports bring out personal proficiency and could be suitable for jobs in research, audit, accounting, etc.
- It evaluates whether you have gone into depth in your sport of choice. It shows your real commitment to the game and the extent to which you learn from it. It applies also to an armchair cricketer!

Q19. "Tell me a time when you failed and what you did to recover."

To err is human. To go through life without failure is impossible. What interviewers are really seeking is the response to such failures. Choose a failure in your life that will be inconsequential to your job. One good answer I received was,

"I lost a crucial tennis tie against a leading college when I was representing my college, and I let them down. As soon as I lost, I went straight to the practice courts to correct some of the mistakes I had made. I concentrated with a single mind to improve my game. I beat my opponent and won the cup for the college the next year. My failure had indeed made me a better person". Wonderful!

Q20. "Why should we select you?"

Treat this as a gift question. Sell yourself completely. Stress on how you are qualified for the job; talk about those personal qualities that will suit the job; reflect on your competencies; and most of all, your goals, aspirations, and motivations. This question should absolutely swing the interview in your favour.

Q21. Tell us about your values as related to the job.

Values are your beliefs that translate into action. Interviewers want to know whether you will be an upright person for the organisation. Some notable values are *honesty, hard work, conscientiousness, teamwork, respect for others, helpfulness, customer orientation, a positive attitude, and being open to critique.* Build your answer around these.

Q22. "What are your career options right now?"

Prepare for this question by thinking of how you can position yourself as a desired 'commodity'. If you are still working, describe the opportunities at your present firm. If you're not working, you can talk about other employment possibilities you're actually exploring. But do this with a light touch, speaking only in general terms. You don't want to seem manipulative or coy.

Q23. "Why have you been out of work for so long?"

You want to emphasise factors that have prolonged your job search by your own choice. Example:

"After my last job, I made a conscious decision not to jump on the first opportunity that came along. I decided to take whatever time I needed to think through what I do best, what I most want to do, and where I'd like to do it, and then identify those companies that could offer such an opportunity. Yours is one of them".

You can use another approach, provided it is true.

"There is a recession in the banking, financial services, manufacturing, advertising, etc.) industry, and finding a job where I can effectively contribute is hard to come by. I do not want to take anything that comes my way".

You can say, *"Once I get a perfect fit for this job in question, I look forward to a long inning".*

Q24. You do not have enough experience in this area.

Before going into any interview, you would have assessed your match for the position. If you fall short of experience, then prepare the best answer you possibly can.

When the interviewer poses such an objection, explain,

"I have other strengths that compensate for this weakness".

Then review the areas of your greatest strengths that match up most favourably with the company's needs.

This is a powerful way to handle this question for two reasons. First, you're sharing your interviewer's concern. But more importantly, you're shifting his focus away from this isolated area and putting it on the unique combination of strengths that tie in perfectly with the company's needs.

Q25. You've been with your firm a long time. Won't it be hard switching to a new company?

Most interviewers are concerned that a 'long-timer' with a company might leverage an offer to secure a better career break with the old company. To overcome this objection, say:

"It has not been a static situation in my present company. I held larger responsibilities as the company grew. They did not give me any reason to leave."

Q26. Why have you changed so many jobs?

This may establish you as a job hopper, which is typically not favoured by companies. However, if you have changed jobs frequently, consider these strategies. First, when composing your resume before the interview stage, try to eliminate job entries that lasted less than a year. Focus on the longer tenures you have served. You can round off the years instead of detailing months. Unfortunately, in today's job market, millennials often change jobs frequently due to the numerous opportunities available. Recruiters are gradually becoming more accepting of the idea of quick attrition.

Example: Instead of showing three positions this way:

Position at XYZ	6/1982 – 4/1983
Position at ABC	8/1983 – 12/1983
Position at MNO	1/1984 – 8/1987

You can simplify it as:

Position at XYZ 1982 – 1983

Position MNO 1984 – 1987

In other words, you have dropped the position at ABC altogether. Notice what a difference this makes in reducing your image as a job hopper. Describe each new company as part of your overall growth plan. You may attribute certain changes to conditions beyond your control. Example:

"There was talk of a merger and that my department would be axed. I made the career change before that eventuality".

Another approach could be:

"I was younger then and unsure of my career path. I was seeking new skills and learning then. I am mature now, know what I want, and am therefore more stable".

Q27. "What good books have you read lately?"

This question is asked to ascertain whether you keep up-to-date with developments and information in the field. It would work to your advantage if you kept reading professional books as a habit to keep you abreast of the latest concepts, jargon, buzz words, etc.

Q28. "May I contact your present employer for a reference?"

Express your concern that you'd like to keep your job search private as you are still employed with them, but in time, it will be perfectly okay.

Q29. "Give me an example of your achievements".

You would have already listed your greatest and most recent achievements during your preparation for the interview. For example, you could have landed your company with a lucrative contract, participated in a trade show that secured new business, or introduced a new concept of marketing in your company.

"What if I have no achievements?" You would have at least met your targets. If that is also not true, then concentrate on achievements in school and college. It is not possible that you have no achievements. It is just that you have not thought about them.

Q30. How could you have improved your career progression?

First, make sure you have a career plan. If your career has been haphazard, then make sure you have logical reasons for making such decisions. For example, uncertain market conditions, a sluggish industry, a force majeure that effected the industry, a pandemic, etc. made you make hasty career decisions.

Stand by your career's progress. Take responsibility for where you are, how you've gotten there, where you are going, and that you harbour no regrets. Emphasise that the position you are interviewing for is a step in the right direction.

Q31. "What interests you about this job?"

The best way to respond is to describe the qualifications listed in the job advertisement and then connect them to your education, skills, and experience. That way, the employer will see that you know about the job you're interviewing for.

Q32. "Tell me about a special project you did."

This is a fabulous way to showcase yourself and your abilities. The human resources person may not be qualified to ask technical questions about many jobs and therefore ask a generalised one such as this. While many technical aspects of the project may fly over the interviewer's head, he or she is actually looking at other things, such as:

- The enthusiasm with which you speak about the project
- The personal qualities that emerged during the project
- Your ability to work in a team
- Your ability to lead a team (if you were the team leader)
- Your time consciousness in completing the task
- How did you plan your work?
- Your system of monitoring and control

- Your quality consciousness
- The number of hours you put into the work
- The innovation you introduced
- The systems and procedures you followed

Go ahead and blow your trumpet.

Q33. "What can you add to what we have already asked you that should make us want to hire you?"

This is the moment of truth. Fill in all the things about yourself that did not emerge during the interview so far.

Think grocery shopping—all those brands in the soap aisle beg for your attention. Each one comes with its own key selling point.

What are your key selling points? This must be planned before the interview. Concentrate on your core strengths. Provide examples, perhaps statistics, and percentages.

Q34. How do you think you have done in this interview?

Such questions are asked to put you on the spot. If you say "well," it may appear boastful, while if you say "not so well," it may cross out your chances of success. The best way to approach this question is to say,

"I think you have been wonderful to get all there is to know about me."

Then add,

"The purpose of my meeting is to give you all the information necessary to determine my suitability for your needs. I feel that by now we both see the common areas of suitability".

Q35. "Do You Have Any Questions?"

There are great questions, dumb questions, and, worst of all, no questions at all.

The interviewer's last question is frequently the most important one. That's when the interviewer smiles and asks it. Your response at this point often determines if you are a job seeker or a job getter.

You cannot succeed in a job interview without asking well-considered questions. It shows you make well-informed decisions. Remember the concept of mutuality at the beginning of the book?

Ask about company training programmes, growth prospects, challenges in the job, onboarding programme (induction), reward and recognition programmes, organisation structure, working hours, company transport on official duty, etc. Don't talk about money and benefits until the interviewer broaches them.

Functional interview questions

Q36. "Why do you consider yourself suitable for the job?"

Functional job interviewers are primarily interested in your qualifications, knowledge, skills, experience, and competencies for the job. HR would have summed up your personality, psychological and emotional make-up, upbringing, values, and motivations to fit the job. While some of these may already be described in your resume, they want to hear your personal testimony. They may throw some functional problems at you and see how you tackle them. Speak with a confident voice. Be short and to the point.

Q37. Aren't you overqualified for this position?

As with any objection, don't view this as a sign of imminent defeat. It's an invitation to teach the interviewer a new way to think about this situation, seeing advantages instead of drawbacks.

"I believe that there could be very positive benefits for both of us in this match. Because of my unusually strong experience, I could start to contribute right away, perhaps much faster than someone who just started his career."

"There's also the value of all the training and years of experience that other companies have invested. You'd be getting all the value of that without having to pay an extra dime for it, as against someone inexperienced."

"I will also always have the potential for higher responsibilities whenever you are ready. It will be an internal promotion rather than having to go back to the market to find someone. You could also use my strengths to

upgrade the staff and bring in the latest practices. I will be the mentor and coach for less experienced teams."

"Most important, I can train the future generation of employees with all the qualifications and experience I have. Also, I am looking to make a long-term commitment to my career now".

The main concern behind the "overqualified" question is the fear that you will leave your new employer as soon as something better comes your way. Anything you can say to demonstrate the sincerity of your commitment to the employer and reassure him that you're looking to stay for the long term will help you overcome this objection.

Q38: "This job is not a bed of roses. Would you still like to join it?"

Interviewers sometimes deliberately paint a gloomy picture to ascertain your real interest in the job. Say,

"I love challenges. The more difficult it is, my best comes out".

Q39. "What are your expectations from the job?"

Interviewers are anxious about whether they will be able to give you job satisfaction. One answer that impressed me was,

"I like a job like yours that will use my qualifications, experience, and talents. I want to be challenged and given additional responsibilities that will help me learn and grow".

In this answer, the candidate showed his enthusiasm to contribute, his willingness to accept challenges, and his desire to learn and grow if he were given additional responsibilities. He was selected.

Q40. "What are some of the things you find difficult to do?"

The interviewer aims to assess your self-awareness, how you handle challenging situations or tasks, your honesty, and the lessons you've learned from such experiences. Examples of personal challenges might include public speaking, disagreeing with a manager on a crucial matter, or being asked to use unfamiliar software. Here's an example of a response to this question:

"I often find that I need a day or two to prepare for presentations to department heads. I tend to get nervous and struggle with spontaneity. However, I've learned that by giving myself time to gather facts, I can present with greater confidence."

Q41. "What do you think makes a good team member?"

Questions like this aim to determine your suitability as a team member. A good response might include the following parameters:

1. *Thoroughly understanding team objectives.*
2. *Recognising each team member's strengths and weaknesses to help compensate for weaknesses.*
3. *Maintaining a friendly and approachable attitude.*
4. *Possessing a deep knowledge of company systems and procedures.*
5. *Understanding local terminology and jargon.*
6. *Complementing the skills of fellow team members.*
7. *Providing assistance to team members during times of stress.*
8. *Sharing information to keep the team well-informed.*
9. *Demonstrating respect towards team members.*
10. *Offering coaching to others while also being receptive to learning from them.*
11. *Upholding the team's commitment to quality and safety.*
12. *Adding value to the team.*
13. *Adhering to the team's disciplinary norms and providing guidance to those who deviate.*
14. *Fostering enthusiasm.*

Q42. "Why do you think we should hire you for this position?"

To answer a question like this, thorough preparation is essential before the interview:

1. Research the job and the organisation, and create a list of the required knowledge, skills, and experience.

2. Evaluate your own skills, experience, competencies, and personal traits in comparison to the job profile.

Create a list with the following headings:

Needs of the new Job	What I can provide

Having matched this sell, yourself by mentioning the benefits of hiring you as the solution to their problem.

Q43. "Describe a challenging work issue you had to face and how you dealt with it?"

You will approach this question through preparation much in the same way as the previous question. Now you will add a new column to the list:

Needs of the new Job	What I can provide	Proof from my past job

By doing this, you can provide examples that directly relate to the new job, which will leave a stronger impression on the interviewer compared to unrelated examples. Preparing these lists can boost your confidence when facing the interview because you will have a clearer understanding of the new job's requirements.

Q44. "How do you handle conflict?"

In a professional setting, conflicts can arise from various sources, such as fellow employees, management, rules and procedures, clients, customers, or the balance between work and personal life. It's essential to approach this question from the employer's perspective, as they value problem solvers rather than problem creators. You can respond with an answer like this:

"I understand that workplace conflicts are inevitable from time to time. When a conflict arises, my approach is to identify the source of the problem and explore potential solutions. I often involve other members of the work team to brainstorm solutions collaboratively. After evaluating the available options, I select the solution that appears to have the most favourable outcome and implement it."

Q45. "Tell me about a time when you tried and failed?"

No one is infallible, and it's important to acknowledge that even interviewers have faced failures. As the saying goes, "to err is human." Interviewers typically appreciate candidates who admit to making mistakes and are interested in their ability to handle and learn from those mistakes. If you have a relevant example, share it along with the lessons you learned from the experience.

Q46. "Tell us about your analytical skills".

Analytical skills use logic and rationale. Make a list of past analysis as proof. From your inventory, who can rattle off some examples?

Q47. "What does customer service mean to you?"

This is an important question for jobs with customer contact. Interviewers want to see how customer-oriented you are. The best way to approach this question is to think of yourself as a customer. Say,

"I'd ask myself what I expect from a salesperson. It is respect, patience, and one who solves my problem or search".

Q48. "What, in your opinion, makes a good supervisor or manager?"

This is a question for those who are aspiring for supervisory or managerial positions (sometimes for the first time). For those who have already had supervisory or managerial experience, the question should not be so difficult. For those who are entering supervisory or managerial positions, here are some tips:

A good supervisor or manager should:

- Be a good leader by balancing tasks and human aspects.
- Set objectives for the team and consult the team on how to achieve them.
- Understand his team members individually, including their strengths and weaknesses.
- Assign responsibilities to the strengths and capabilities of each team member.

- Be a good listener.
- Coach his team members.
- Command respect by being firm yet fair.
- Recognise good work in public and reprimand it in private.
- Help the team members grow.
- Be aware of the aspirations of team members and guide them towards their goals.
- Protect team members from external threats.
- Be hands-on during a crisis.
- Be inspirational.
- Maintain the code of conduct.
- Ensure that team members meet quality standards.
- Ensure that the work methods used are safe.
- Show empathy when dealing with team members' personal problems.
- Praise in public, reprimand in privacy.
- Counsel employees and act as a mentor to them.
- Use delegation as a tool of development while maintaining accountability.

Caselets:

You may be presented with small caselets that will demonstrate your supervisory or managerial style, such as:

1. Two employees come to you about a verbal disagreement. One says the incident happened one way, and the other employee has a different story. There are no other witnesses. What will you do?
2. You have an exemplary employee who suddenly starts coming in late. How will you handle this situation?

3. You supervise a group of employees; one employee complains that the office is too hot; another employee complains that the office is too cold. How will you handle this?

4. An employee complains that you gave another employee a benefit that the employee did not receive. He states that this is not fair. How will you handle this employee?

5. A supervisor from another group comes to you and complains that your employee visits the other group constantly and disrupts the work. What steps will you take?

Use the principles of a good supervisor or manager when answering these caselets. Interviewers are more interested in the principles you will use than the solution itself.

Q49: "Tell me honestly about the strong and weak points of your boss (company, management team, etc.)"

Remember a golden rule: Never be negative about your previous boss or company. Stress only the good points, no matter how charmingly you're invited to be critical.

Your future boss could well be sitting on this interview panel, if not the only person interviewing you.

Q50. "Tell me about a situation when your work was criticised."

Begin by emphasising the extremely positive feedback you've gotten throughout your career and (if it's true) that your performance reviews have been uniformly excellent. Also, assure me that you value critique, as it helps you improve and perform better.

Q51. "How do you feel about reporting to a younger person (minority, woman, etc.)?"

Say, "*I believe in equal opportunity and greatly admire a company that hires and promotes on merit alone, and you couldn't agree more with that philosophy. The age, gender, race, etc. of the person you report to would certainly make no difference to me*".

Q52. "What would you say to your boss if you disagree with his idea?"

In any conflict between values, always choose integrity. You can say,

"I believe that integrity overrides anything else. It is my job to point out things that may seem dishonest and will impact the boss and department. In terms of job-related matters, I will point them out in a constructive way, as specifically, objectively, and factually as I can. I owe my boss my honesty. If he still goes ahead after my input, I will respect and support him; after all, he has a broader picture. I am sure my boss will consider my point of view".

Q53. "What would you do if a colleague was not performing that affects your department?"

Just say, *"I'll coach him."*

POSSIBLE FOLLOW-UP QUESTION:

Q54. "And what would you do if he still did not change his ways?"

Answer by saying,

"One thing I wouldn't do is let the problem slide, because it would only get worse. I would counsel him or her and recommend further training involving others if necessary. If the problem persists, I will recommend a hard decision, which may include the termination of service. After all, the performance of the company must not suffer."

"I might add that I've never yet come across a situation that couldn't be resolved by harnessing others in a determined, constructive effort."

Interviewers want to see if you have the guts to take hard decisions if needed.

Q55. What are the areas that you can improve upon?

Choose an area that is not threatening to your employer's needs. Tell them the steps that you have already taken and how excited you are about the improvements. Examples can be a new technology introduced or how to participate in a trade show.

Q56. How do you feel about working late and on weekends?

Remember that modern work environments demand long hours, sometimes on weekends. This is particularly true of the service industry, like BPOs, banks, hotels, etc. If you're a confirmed workaholic, say,

"This kind of schedule is just my style. My family supports me".

If, however, you prefer a more balanced lifestyle, say,

"A smart performer finishes his work in the allotted time. This means that his productivity is high. Am I one of them? However, I believe in job completion, and if I am required to work extra hours sometimes, then I will do so on my own."

If the timing just does not suit you, say so, but phrase your response positively.

"I do have a family who likes to see me after work and on weekends. They add balance and richness to my life, which in turn helps me be productive at work. If I could handle some of the extra work at home, where I can be under the same roof as my family, Everybody would win."

Q57: "Do you have the stomach to fire people?"

Say: *"My whole management approach is to hire the best people, train them thoroughly, get them excited and proud to be part of our team, and then work with them to achieve our goals together. I believe that if you do all of that right, especially hiring the right people, you don't have to fire very often. However, if it is the last resort, I'll do it".*

Q58. "Could you have done better in your last job?"

Don't be negative. You can say something like this:

"I suppose with the benefit of hindsight you can always find things to do better, of course, but off the top of my head, I can't think of anything of major consequence."

If they press for an incident, then choose one with the fewest consequences.

Q59. "Describe a situation when you suffered from conditions beyond your control."

Treat this as an opportunity to bring out your strengths under difficult circumstances. You can say something like this:

"I had prepared a beautiful PowerPoint presentation for a business client to clinch a lucrative contract. On that day, the power went out, and I was left to make the presentation verbally. Thank goodness I have good communication skills, logical thinking, and the ability to stay calm. I had also planned the presentation thoroughly. I gave the presentation verbally under a dim emergency light. We got the contract!"

Q60. "Can you work under pressure?"

There is no other answer but "yes." You can say,

"I love the adrenalin rush under pressure. The more it is, the better I perform".

Then prove it with a real-life example.

Q61. "What was the toughest decision you ever had to make?"

Be prepared with a good example, explaining why the decision was difficult, the process you followed in reaching it, the courageous or effective way you carried it out, and the beneficial results.

Q62. "Tell me about the most boring job you've ever had."

Claim that you have never allowed yourself to grow bored with a job, and you can't understand it when others let themselves fall into that rut. Say,

"Perhaps I've been fortunate not to be bored with any job. I've always looked for creative challenges requiring energetic and enthusiastic solutions. I prefer to go to my boss for more duties and responsibilities than let my job get routine".

Q63. "What do you look for when you hire people?"

This could be asked of you if one of your job components is to hire people. Obviously, you would like to state the obvious:

Is he or she qualified for the position? (Academic attainment, experience, personality traits, competencies, and skills)

Is s/he motivated?

Will s/he culturally fit into our organisation?

Is s/he a team player?

Does s/he show potential to grow?

Q64. "Sell me this stapler".

This is a question often asked of those who have a direct sales role.

The most important secret of salesmanship is "to find out what people want and then show them how the product fits that want."

To do this, a good salesman must know both his product (its features and benefits) and his prospect before he sells anything.

Then proceed to ask questions to establish the 'buyers' needs. Some questions you can ask are:

"What specific use will you have for it?"

"What features are you looking for?"

"Are you particular about a colour or will anyone do?"

"Are you particular about the brand name?"

"Is there anything else?"

Give suggestions:

"Would you like it to be reliable?"

"Would you like it to be small and compact?"

"Would you like the staples to be easily available?"

"Wouldn't you like a stapler that can use any brand of staples?"

Once you've asked these questions, make your presentation citing all the features and benefits of this stapler and why it's exactly what the interviewer just told you he's looking for.

Then close with, "Just out of curiosity, what would you consider a reasonable price for a quality stapler like this?" Whatever he says (unless it's zero), say, "Okay, we've got a deal."

Tip: You would be most likely asked to'sell' items that are often found on an office desk! (e.g., pen, desk calendar, desk clock, etc.)

Q65. "Have you been absent from work more than a few days in any previous position?"

Say,

"I have had an excellent and consistent attendance record throughout my career, except when I had the flu for three days, which was beyond my control. I believe consistent attendance keeps the operation running smoothly".

Q66. "What changes would you make if you came on board?"

A good answer would be:

"Well, I wouldn't be a very good doctor if I gave my diagnosis before the examination of the patient. Should you hire me, I'd want to understand thoroughly the nature of the work and why it's being done that way. I'd like to conduct in-depth meetings with you and the other key people to get a deeper grasp of what you feel you're doing right and what could be improved. The solution is a collective decision".

Another way to answer this question is to ask,

"Are there any specific concerns you have?"

If stated, proceed to ask them relevant questions. It is the kind of questions you ask rather than the solution you give that is important. The interviewer will evaluate whether you are asking the right questions. Use questions starting with *where, what, why, when, and how!*

Q67. "How many hours a week do you normally work?"

This is a question to evaluate whether you are a clock-watcher or flexible with time to get the job done. Say,

"I believe in job completion. It is more important to me than the hours of work put in".

Q68. "What's the most difficult part of being in this position?"

Say,

"I wouldn't call it "difficult" but "challenging". As a receptionist, I find rush hours a challenge. I just keep my mind alert and be to the point with the inquiries.

Q69: "What was the toughest challenge you've ever faced?"

This is an easy question if you're prepared. Have a recent example ready that demonstrates a quality most important to the job.

Q70. "Why should we hire you instead of promoting someone from within?"

This is a perennial question facing every organisation: hire from outside or promote from within. Well, obviously, professional organisations would have career plans and, in some cases, succession plans for critical positions. The general rule is to promote from within. There are many reasons why organisations seek people from outside. These reasons can be used as your arguments for this question:

- No internal qualified employee
- Growing fast, requiring additional people on board
- Want fresh ideas coming into the organisation
- We need an objective person to lead a team.
- Shortage of qualified manpower
- Vacancies are greater than those on board.
- Changes in organisation structures
- Entered into a new product range
- Opened business in a new geographical area
- Introduced a new technology or process

- It is a start-up company.
- Attrition of staff is faster than input.
- Sudden vacancies

Help the interviewer see the qualifications that only you can offer. Say,

"In general, I think it's a good policy to hire from within. Obviously, you have given it your first thought and still want to see options outside. I am here to add value to your operations. Maybe my contributions will help add new dimensions".

Q71. "What kind of boss do you prefer?"

This is a tricky question, as your future boss sitting on the interview panel could be the opposite of what you desire. If he is, then it is just as well that you do not join the organisation. One good answer I received was,

"Every boss wants someone to bring hurrahs to him as the leader and the team. He recognises performance and gives me the flexibility to use my talents and creativity within the broad guidelines of policies and procedures. I see my boss as a partner, and my objective is to see him succeed. In partnership, there is open communication, and we solve problems together".

I found this answer spectacular, as it clearly stated the objective as the boss's success. This will disarm any boss.

Q72. "What are your expectations from the job?"

There isn't a right or wrong answer to this question. The best way to respond is to discuss what you expected when you took the job and give examples of how the position worked out for you. If the job wasn't exactly what you expected, it's fine to mention that. However, you should focus on the job itself, not the company, your boss, or your co-workers (if they were a problem). Be careful how you answer, and don't focus too much on the negative. Instead, address the highlights of the job.

When responding, be specific. Prepare some examples to share with the interviewer in advance.

Q73. "What are your present duties and responsibilities?"

When you are asked questions related to your current or previous positions, it's important to be specific and positive about what you did. Try to relate it to the job you are interviewing for.

It's also important to be honest. Don't embellish your job because you don't know who the hiring manager will be checking with when they speak to your references.

Q74. "How do you handle challenges?"

Say,

"I analyse the challenge thoroughly and try to find the best solution".

Give an example.

Q75. "What was the most and least interesting part of your job?"

Say,

"Whenever I sense the job is getting routine, I go to my boss for new responsibilities to make the job interesting. He starts delegating some tasks to keep my job interesting."

Q76. "What was the biggest accomplishment in your present or last position?"

Your potential employer wants to see how high you raise your bar of accomplishment.

An accomplishment could be a consistent above-average rating in your performance appraisal, winning the 'Best Employee of the Month' recognition, achieving a great contract, customer appreciation to the management, etc.

Q77. "What was it like working for your supervisor?"

This is a follow-up trap question to Q.49. The reason this question is asked is to ascertain your consistency in your relationship with the boss. Speak glowingly about the relationship you had with your boss, even if you had the worst experience with him or her. Bring out the qualities you liked most and suggest what you would like your new boss to do, such as individual development, flexibility to use your initiative, setting standards of performance and training you to those standards, etc.

Q78. "How do you handle stress?"

This is a typical question to ascertain how you handle on-the-job stress. Examples of good responses include:

- *"Stress is very important to me. With stress, I do the best possible job. The appropriate way to deal with stress is to make sure I have the correct balance between good stress and bad stress. I need good stress to stay motivated and productive".*
- *"I actually work better under pressure".*
- *"From a personal perspective, I manage stress by visiting the gym every evening. It's a great stress reducer".*
- *"I prioritise my responsibilities so I have a clear idea of what needs to be done first to create an impact on my job.*
- *"If the people I am managing are contributing to my stress level, I discuss options for better handling difficult situations with them".*

It's a good idea to give examples of how you have handled stress to your interviewer.

Q79. "What motivates you?"

There isn't a right or wrong answer to interview questions about what motivates you. The interviewer is trying to understand the key to your being successful in the job you are interviewing for and wants to make sure it's a good fit. Consider, in advance, what actually motivates you and come up with some specific examples to share during the interview.

- Here are some examples:
- "I like taking responsibility and being made accountable for it".

- "I found I was good at heading development projects. The teams I led achieved 100% on-time delivery of software products. I was motivated both by the challenge of finishing the projects ahead of schedule and by managing the teams that achieved our goals".
- "I've always been motivated by the desire to do a good job at whatever position I'm in".

Q80. "What religion do you follow?"

This is an illegal question. Illegal questions are those that deny you equal opportunity. They really are not related to your ability to perform the job. Illegal questions can include (based on the state):

- Your age
- Number and ages of your children or other dependents
- Marital status
- Maiden name
- Religion
- Political affiliation
- Ancestry
- National origin
- Birthplace
- Naturalisation of your parents
- Income of your parents
- Spouses or children
- Diseases
- Disabilities
- Membership in clubs (unless professional clubs)
- Spouse's occupation.

Interviewers are aware of these taboo questions out of fear of lawsuits. Yet you may encounter untrained interviewers who may ask such questions. You can handle an illegal question by saying:

"Excuse me. I wish to assert my legal right not to answer".

Or "Pardon me, sir! I wish to keep my personal life private."

Q81. "On a scale of one to ten, rate me as an interviewer."

This is a question asked by untrained interviewers who want feedback on their own performance to improve in the future. Don't be negative. The interviewer will only resent criticism coming from you. This is the time to show your positivism.

You can say, *"You have been thorough in getting to know me."*

In other words, pay him a sincere compliment. Give him a "ten" if he insists on a numerical figure. You lose nothing!

Q82. "Tell me something innovative you have introduced at your workplace."

Remember that an organisation survives on the innovative ideas of its people to get a competitive edge. Innovation has become the cornerstone of performance management systems. Your best bet to secure a job is the innovation that you bring with you. Interviewers may overlook other negative aspects if you are going to energise the organisation with new ideas. (Just make sure that you have new ideas; otherwise, you are out of the job market!).

Final interview questions

Q83. "What do you know about our company?"

This question is to evaluate your real interest in the organisation. It brings out the preparation you have done to learn about the company. The interviewer believes that your interest in a company can only stem from your knowledge about it. A candidate's blank about the company or their sketchy knowledge is only driven by monetary gains. If you can relate your knowledge in addition to the area that you would be involved in, it would show the depth of your interest. For example, if you were interested in marketing,

"I understand that you are one of the top 10 companies in sales to Asia but are currently interested in expanding your market into Europe. Competition is fierce in that area, but you have an advantage in that your product offers features that others do not, such as..."

It shows that you have done genuine research. You will secure the job.

Q84. Describe your ideal company, location, and job.

The question is asked to ascertain your commitment to the organisation and whether the organisation can hold you for a long time. One good answer I received was,

"I am looking for a challenge to make another promising company like yours maintain your market leadership".

Another example you can give is:

"I am more interested in job content and what I can contribute to the company. I feel that I will get that opportunity in your company".

Q85. "Are you willing to go where the organisation sends you?"

Senior management of companies with multi-geographic locations wants to have the benefit of deploying their good workers according to their business needs. In recent times, the question of mobility has become critical. I find that people are reluctant to move out of a chosen location on three counts:

1. Inflation has necessitated that the wife work in order to supplement the family income. Some wives are career-minded and have responsible jobs as well. Very often, the wife has a good income. This freezes mobility, as it means splitting the family.
2. Housing has become an acute problem due to high rentals. Many opt to stay in a location because they own a house and prefer staying in it for various reasons. They are unwilling to uproot themselves.
3. Children's education is an acute problem since admission into schools is very difficult.

4. People are familiar with a city and have family and friend networks in the city. They are unwilling to move to unfamiliar surroundings.

If these criteria influence you, then it is best to state your inability to move, given the above reasons. It is possible that your growth may be slower than that of those who take risks with mobility. But that is the choice you will have to make. I have found many candidates blindly saying "yes" to the question to secure the job, only to find themselves in a quandary when asked to move later. It is unfair to the organisation.

Q86. "What do you wish to gain from our company?"

Excellent question! The answer lies in your research of the organisation. Just remember that your answer to this question can land you the job since it is the final interview. Determine some of the key elements in the corporate structure, product base, employees, management team, or recent history. What appeals to you about working at this company? Go with what you know.

Here is a good answer:

"In the past, I have had opportunities to work on new products being launched. I am very excited about your plans to start an entire new product line. With my prior experience, I know I can provide insights and make contributions immediately, and I will also learn so much from the excellent team you have in place".

Find something specific that hooks you. E.g., the opportunity to use a new technology, a new skill, to work with experts on their team, a new market, cutthroat competition that makes your adrenaline rush, the element of risk, etc.

Q87. "What do you think are the employee's responsibilities to the company?"

As an employee, you have several responsibilities to your employer. They are as follows:

- Bring in innovation.
- Perform a good day's work.

- ✲ Be loyal and honest.
- ✲ Add value
- ✲ Earn the employer's trust.
- ✲ Display genuine ownership of the company's products and services.
- ✲ Help the organisation grow.
- ✲ Promote the company in the marketplace and social circles.
- ✲ Solve problems
- ✲ Help in achieving the objectives of the organisation
- ✲ Exceed the expectations of the organisation
- ✲ Help fulfil the organisation's commitments.

Senior management wants to be assured that you will be a responsible and reliable corporate citizen of the company.

Q88. "Give me some confidential information about your company.

The interviewer may not ask such a blatant question but may do so subtly through other means. He or she may press you for this information for two reasons: 1) Many companies use interviews to research the competition. It's a perfect setup. Here in their own lair is an insider from the enemy camp who can reveal prized information on the competition's plans, research, financial condition, etc. 2) The company may be testing your integrity to see if you can be cajoled or bullied into revealing confidential data.

Be alert. Never reveal anything truly confidential about a present or former employer. By all means, explain your reticence diplomatically. For example,

"I certainly want to be as open as I can about that. But I also wish to respect the rights of those who have trusted me with their most sensitive information, just as you would hope to be able to trust any of your key people when talking with a competitor".

doesn't get it, he grows visibly annoyed and relentlessly inquisitive. It's all an act. He couldn't care less about the information. This is his way of testing the candidate's moral fibre. Only those who hold fast are hired.

Q89. "Would you lie for the company?"

You may say, *"I would never do anything to hurt the company."*

If aggressively pressed to choose between two competing values, always choose personal integrity. It is the most prized of all values.

Q90. "Have you considered starting your own business?"

This is a double-edged sword. It tells whether you will learn from the company and start your own business, becoming a direct competitor, or whether you have the entrepreneurial spirit desired by most modern organisations.

You might say, "Oh, I may have given it a thought once or twice, but my whole career has been in larger organisations. That's where I have excelled and where I want to be."

Q91. "What are your goals?"

To be a professional means setting goals. Interviewers like to see evidence of that. The interviewers would be strong believers in goal-setting. It's one of the reasons they've achieved so much. They like to hire in kind.

If you're vague about your career and personal goals, it could be a big turnoff to many people you will encounter in your job search.

Be ready to discuss your goals for each major area of your life: career, personal development and learning, family, physical health, and community service.

Be prepared to describe each goal in terms of specific milestones you wish to accomplish along the way, time periods you're allotting for accomplishment, why the goal is important to you, and the specific steps you're taking to bring it about.

This question will need preparation and practice. It should be concise. Remember, they are your goals and cannot be judged as right or wrong.

Q92. "Tell me something negative you've heard about our company."

Just remember the rule—never be negative—and you'll handle this one just fine. Reconfirm all the good things about the company that attract you.

Q93. "What are your criteria for selecting an organisation?"

The purpose of this question is to evaluate whether your goals can be fulfilled by the organisation. Senior management can expect you to leave if they cannot satisfy your needs. Some acceptable criteria used by most organisations are:

1. Organisation **growth,** which will foster personal growth and advancement While growth relates to any new experience that gives you more skills and knowledge, advancement is the progression in responsibilities and titles.
2. Opportunity to be **innovative** All organisations these days value innovation because of the fast pace at which new ideas are introduced.
3. **Recognition** of work well done Anybody likes to be rewarded financially and otherwise for a job well done.
4. The work **culture** of the organisation should be professional and progressive. The ability to communicate freely with superiors is important to bring about better understanding at the workplace.

Q94. "How do you evaluate success?"

Say, *"The organisation's success is my success, and vice versa. My key result areas must lead to the organisation's progress and prosperity".*

Q95. "What kind of rewards do you value most?"

This question is very similar to the earlier one. Your reward is when the organisation succeeds. The organisation's success will naturally lead to individual rewards. One good answer I received was,

"I value making the organisation succeed first. Its success will automatically generate rewards for me in kind and recognition".

Q96. "What three factors are most valuable to you in your job?"

This question is asked to see whether your values lead to organisation success. The three factors that will be acceptable to them are: teamwork, quality job completion, and customer orientation. Other noteworthy factors can be profitability through cost control, productivity, loyalty to the organisation and profession, continuous improvement, new knowledge and skills, and exceeding customer service.

Q97. "Which work environment are you most comfortable working in?"

Senior interview panellists are anxious about whether their work organisation is conducive to getting the best out of you. You would have already found out about the organisation's work culture in your preparation for the interview. You can then use the exact factors that the organisation offers to give your candidature a perfect fit. However, if you have been unable to get the desired information about the organisation then you can use a generalised statement like,

"My best environment is one that gives expression to my talents and skills".

Q98. "What have you done to improve yourself?"

This is a question to ascertain whether you are engaged in continuous education. There are those who wait for the organisation to train and develop them. They are happy to wait until it happens. Such candidates are often left obsolete. There are others who are proactive and invest in training programmes to improve, trade periodicals, and web inquiries.

There is a new acronym these days called **FOMO,** or Fear of Being Obsolete. Change today is happening very fast, and one has to keep up to date.

Q99. "Where do you see yourself in ten years?"

Make sure that you emphasise that you see yourself with the company in ten years! This will show your commitment to the organisation. Also, choose a position that is achievable for you—maybe in middle or senior management. It shows your ambition and the confidence to reach there. Nobody is going to take stock after ten years of whether you reached where you wanted to be. So shoot for the sky. One flattering answer I received was,

"Sir, I would hope to be sitting on the other side of this interview table like you one day!"

The Compensation Interview Questions

Q100. What were the starting and ending levels of your compensation?

Interviewers ask this question to evaluate how you progressed in your performance, adding value to your compensation package. They can make the difference between marginal increments that compensate for the extra year you put in with the company and those superlative jumps in salary showing your outstanding performance. They will also understand a jump in salary when changing jobs. This adequately explains your motive to change jobs.

Interviewers expect you to be able to provide the details of their compensation history. Be prepared for this. Don't exaggerate or inflate your earnings. Many employers will check references and confirm your salary history prior to making a job offer. A discrepancy between what you reported and what the employer says could knock you out of contention for the job.

Q.101. "What are your salary expectations?"

This embarrassing question can be met with preparation. Some jobs advertised have a salary range. If you have applied, that means that you are comfortable with that range. Other jobs state 'salary negotiable, which then requires you to be adept at salary negotiation. The first step is to ask yourself the following question:

How much am I worth?

Your value is based on the market for such positions. You can get this information by several means: a) scanning the job advertisements in the daily newspaper or other published job sites. b) Consult recruitment agents who know the value of various jobs in different industries. Some agents are industry-specific and would have even done some compensation studies of the industry. c) Check some public compensation surveys found in the town library; d) Ask past and present employees in the organisation you are applying to and find out what they are paying for such positions.

Based on your skills and experience, you can decide whether you want to be the leader on the salary scale, at the midpoint of the scale, or at the entry level. Be realistic with yourself and pitch yourself accordingly. Those who pitch themselves at the highest point are obviously extremely talented and have a proven track record of achievement. They have confidence to fulfil the higher expectations of the organisation. Remember that any compensation brings corresponding levels of performance expectations. Organisations are willing to pay well for a good candidate because they expect a higher rate of return from their investment in the candidate. Do not be greedy because you will have to be able to give an A-one performance. I have found that those given high salaries are watched carefully by the management. They are always evaluating whether that cost is paying back in performance.

Changing jobs for the sake of compensation means that it has to be a worthwhile jump. A 25–30% hike is reasonable. Some candidates move jobs for various reasons other than compensation, such as a bigger organisation, more professional organisation, better job fit, better growth prospects, a growth-oriented company, a better work culture, a workplace closer to home, etc. Evaluate what your motivations are for the change. You may want to take a lower salary for better leaps in compensation within the organisation in the future.

Salaries may also change with location. The salary of a job position in a small town may differ substantially from the same position in a large city because the cost of living differs. Similarly, international assignments have different ballparks than domestic jobs. They are benchmarked with prevalent dollar salaries.

NEGOTIATING YOUR SALARY

Once you know what you *should* be earning, how do you go about getting it? Start by being very patient. When interviewing for a new position, do your best not to bring up compensation until the employer makes you an offer. Never bring up salary. Let the interviewer do it first. Good salespeople sell their products thoroughly before talking about price. So should you. Make the interviewer want you first, and your bargaining position will be much stronger. If you're asked what your salary requirements are,

"I am open based upon the responsibilities and the overall compensation package."

If your interviewer raises the salary question too early, say,

"Money is important to me, but my growth is far more important. What I'd rather do, if you don't mind, is explore if I'm right for the position and its prospects, and then talk about money. Would that be okay?"

The secret is to get the employer talking about what he's willing to pay before you reveal what you're willing to accept. So, when asked about salary, respond by asking,

"I'm sure the company has already established a salary range for this position. Could you tell me what that is?"

Or,

"I want an income commensurate with my ability and qualifications. I trust you'll be fair with me. What does the position pay?"

Or, more simply,

"What does this position pay? It will help me make a decision."

Be aware of the salary restrictions of the new organisation. They may not want to give you more than others in similar positions. If they are rigid, then there is nothing you can do but refuse the job. If they are flexible, then here are a few strategies to overcome this problem:

- These days, companies offer a lump-sum payment called **CTC**, or Cost to Company, for you to break up for your tax planning. (*See para below for more on CTC.*)
- Suggest a new title to get you out of the rut of comparisons. A 'sales agent', for example, can be called a 'sales officer' or 'sales executive'.
- Negotiate for other benefits instead of a direct salary. It could be an entertainment allowance, use of a company car, furnishing allowance, etc.
- Alter the job description marginally to make a difference in role content to warrant higher compensation.
- Do some work for other companies in the same group, getting them to compensate you partially from their books of accounts.
- Work on a commission basis to earn extra for better performance.

Sometimes refusing an offer gets you a counteroffer. You can only take this gamble if 1) you are currently employed and 2) you know that you have done well in the interview and the organisation would like to really have you. It comes to the issue of your self-worth. Simply refuse if it does not meet your benchmark. Usually, you don't have to make a decision about the offer immediately. Ask the employer for a couple of days so you can carefully consider the position and the offer.

Always give them a window to come back by saying,

"I shall let you know within a week".

Another approach is to state your last or present salary and say that you expect a substantially higher jump to motivate you. Most executives look for a 25–30% pay boost when they switch jobs. If you're grossly underpaid, you may want more. Never lie about what you currently make, but feel free to include the estimated cost of all your fringes, which could well tack on 25–50% more to your present "cash-only" salary.

If this question is asked, do not feel bashful, but state your expectations boldly, as it is your right to do so. It is important for you to prepare rationally and logically for what you are expecting.

When weighing the financial terms of salary, see the benefits offered by the organisation. They translate into indirect money. Such benefits are:

- Medical benefits (whether for yourself or your family)
- Transportation
- Housing or allowance
- Canteen and subsidised meals (hotels give free-duty meals)
- Group insurance
- Superannuation benefits
- Entertainment allowance or reimbursement
- Class of travel and accommodation on a tour or vacation
- Annual leave, annual leave fares, leave pay
- Other leave: casual, medical, and emergency
- Relocation expenses

Your base salary and performance-based raises are typically the most negotiable components of your compensation package. However, many companies offer a cafeteria-style approach to benefits, where employees can choose from various benefit options based on a total monetary cost. This approach is commonly referred to as 'Cost to Company' or CTC. In essence, the company allocates a specific amount of money for each employee's benefits, and employees have some flexibility in selecting their preferred benefit options. For instance, employees with children may opt for family medical reimbursement benefits, while those focused on continuous improvement might choose tuition reimbursement, and so on.

If you do reach an agreement with the employer, inquire about the timeline for receiving the offer in writing. It is crucial to obtain an official offer letter before resigning from your current company. An official

"Letter of Offer" signifies the company's commitment to hiring you. If they mention that they will provide you with the appointment letter only after you join, politely request an offer letter, explaining that it would give you the confidence to resign from your current organisation. They should understand the importance of this request.

About the Author

Distinguished Professor, Sudhir Andrews is a graduate of B.A. English (Hons) from St. Stephens College; an MBA from the Indian Institute of Management, Ahmedabad; and a Doctor of Literature from Colombo Open University.

He is the best-selling author of 11 hospitality textbooks, which are used by all hotel schools and universities in India and abroad. He is a Thought Leader and futurist.

He is a best-selling author of 11 Hospitality textbooks which are used by all hotel schools and universities in India and abroad. He is a Thought Leader and Futurist.

He has diverse experience in both the private and public sectors in India and abroad in corporate management (as director) and Education (Principal, Director and Dean); National Hospitality Boards; journalism in India and abroad; lecture tours on career Counselling; as a guest speaker on media; and assignments with the ILO, UNDP, and WTO.

For his contributions, he has won the following awards:

- Rashtriya Gaurav Award
- Rajiv Gandhi Award for Excellence
- Best Citizen of India Award
- International Achievement Award
- All India Business and Excellence Award for Educational Excellence
- International Status Award for Educational Education

- Sri Ram Award for the Best Management Thought
- Hospitality Legendary Award
- Life-Time Achievement Award

He has travelled globally and has vast interviewing knowledge of human resources from all over the world. He brings all his national and international experiences to his writings. He has interviewed knowledge from those entering the job market to those at senior levels; international and national human resources; manufacturing and service industries; and on the panel at the first, second, and third stages of interviews.

Sudhir Andrews has now dedicated his remaining life to helping people succeed in their careers through his writings.

Bibliography

1. Teena Rose – 'Getting Up the Ladder – Getting Ahead on the Job'
2. Alison Doyle- 'Your Guide to Job Searching'
3. Laura Schnieder – 'Your Guide to Technical Careers'
4. Joyce Lain Kennedy – 'Job Interviews for Dummies'
5. Naukri.com
6. Matt and Nan DeLuca – 'Best Answers to 201 Most Frequently Asked Interview Questions'

www.ingramcontent.com/pod-product-compliance
Lightning Source LLC
LaVergne TN
LVHW041215150826
845673LV00001B/405

* 9 7 9 8 8 9 1 3 3 6 3 7 7 *